'*Turned by Divine Love* is a gentle, most accessible ~~~ ~ook
destined, I reckon, to become a cla~~~~ ~ct
honestly about our own willi ~d
by… Divine Love, and provides ~l
nourishment for the journey.'
Brother Stuart Burns OSB, Mucknell Abbe

'This beautifully written book is full ~ ~iscovery of who
we are and who God is. Amid our ~~ and longings, we are invited
to see in new ways and to glimpse afresh what it means to be people of
relationship, made in the image of God, who is love and with whom there are
endless new beginnings.'
The Right Reverend Rachel Treweek, Bishop of Gloucester

'Bishop John has woven his own reflections with insights from other wise
friends of God to refresh hope and draw us into the beauty and depth of faith.
Sustaining, moving, challenging and refreshing, this book draws us into the
depth and beauty of faith. I hope many will read, pray and live it.'
The Right Reverend Alison White, Bishop of Hull

'In this book, John Stroyan… refreshes the old and gives new life to what
has aged. That this is the gift of a contemplative teacher and a bishop in the
church of our time is itself a source of hope and a wonderfully surprising cause
to celebrate.'
Laurence Freeman OSB

'This is a wonderful book and is ideal for anyone wanting to refresh or deepen
their spiritual life. It could also usefully be given to anyone wanting to find
their way into prayer in the first place. It has reflections of a sensibly short
length with questions that lead naturally into the reader's own reflections and
prayer. Attractively written, it is rich in quotation from a wide range of sources.'
The Right Reverend the Lord Harries of Pentregarth

'This is a book full of wisdom. There is unexpected wisdom in the rich selection
of texts that Bishop John has included, from authors ancient and modern,
eastern and western; but there is wisdom also in the perceptive comments of
Bishop John himself… Many readers will certainly find, as I have done, that
here is a book which evokes a "healing fountain" in the depths of their heart.'
The Most Reverend Metropolitan Kallistos Ware of Diokleia

The Bible Reading Fellowship
15 The Chambers, Vineyard
Abingdon OX14 3FE
brf.org.uk

The Bible Reading Fellowship (BRF) is a Registered Charity (233280)

ISBN 978 0 85746 750 8
First published 2019
10 9 8 7 6 5 4 3 2 1 0
All rights reserved

Text © John Stroyan 2019
This edition © The Bible Reading Fellowship 2019
Cover images: *The Return* batik © Solomon Raj; background texture © Thinkstock
Inside images: copyright information can be found on page 128

The author asserts the moral right to be identified as the author of this work

Acknowledgements

Turned by Divine Love

Starting again with God and with others

JOHN STROYAN

BRF

To Mary

Contents

Turn me and I shall be turned.

JEREMIAH 31:18 (GW)

Acknowledgements

The reflections that follow are, inevitably, the fruit of life and ministry in a wide variety of contexts over many years. A common strand running through them is the ecumenical one and the conviction, expressed by Pope John Paul II, that 'the church needs to learn to breathe again with its two lungs – its eastern one and its western one'. My own inner life and ministry has been particularly enriched by considerable contact with the Orthodox Church in this country and overseas, not least on Mount Athos. In this country, a rich gift to me over the past 20 years has been a growing friendship with the Stavropegic Monastery of St John the Baptist in Essex, a place where God is truly worshipped and encountered, not least through the praying of the Jesus Prayer. I am most grateful to the Abbot, Archimandrite Kyrill, for his warm and gracious hospitality over so many years and to Father Zacharias for his friendship and inspiration. I am, in turn, most grateful to Paul Hunt, a true friend in Christ, who introduced me to the monastery and with whom I have been meeting as 'Companions on the Way' for many years. It was Paul who invited me to lead with him the retreat in the Sinai desert.

Another friend, whom I have been privileged to know, is Dr Solomon Raj, a pastor of the Protestant Andhra Evangelical Lutheran Church in India and an inspirational artist. Solomon's batiks and woodcuts on Christian themes have touched and inspired many lives not only in India but across the world. I commissioned the batik on the front cover with the brief to depict the tenderness of God's unconditional love to all who turn to him. I am most grateful to Solomon for permission to use his work in this publication.

A more recent source of inspiration has been the ecumenical Monastic Community of Bose, a place of joy, hospitality and spiritual and ecumenical renewal. The community of brothers and sisters at

Bose, many of them young, attract so many to faith and renewal. I am especially grateful to Sister Elisa for permission to use icons and images from their workshop, and to Sister Lara whose work they are.

Closer to home, I would like to thank Christopher, Bishop of Coventry, and the Diocese of Coventry for the sabbatical space (May–July 2017) in which I was able to do this writing. Even closer to home, I would like to thank Kerry Vanston-Rumney, my PA, who has gone the extra mile again and again, helping with sourcing quotations and copyright. Finally, I would like to thank my wife, Mary, to whom I dedicate this work.

Preface

In returning and rest you shall be saved; in quietness and in trust shall be your strength. But you refused.
ISAIAH 30:15

These words were written probably in the late eighth century BC. At that time, we find the people of Judah under attack from Assyria. In the face of this attack and their obvious vulnerability, they are looking to Egypt for help. In place of seeking and trusting the wisdom of God, they are devising their own plans without reference to God. They are looking for the 'protection of Pharaoh'. In a crisis, it is always tempting, and perhaps even our default mode, to do the same: to look for solutions without seeking first the wisdom of God. We might do so because 'realism dictates...' or 'experience suggests...' or because we think we know best. Any such rationale reveals that we do not have the faith truly to listen to and trust God. Then, when we have made our plans without reference to God, we ask God to bless them.

One of the wonderful things about the Christian faith is that it is all about starting again. It is not just about the first time we turned to Christ, however pivotal and decisive that was in our life's journey. It is about starting again each day. Jesus calls us to take up our cross *each day* and to follow him. Anthony the Great began each day with the words 'Today, I begin again.' This book is about starting again. But this starting again is not just once in prayer at the beginning of each day. It is about the continual movement of turning and returning to God. Francis de Sales wrote to his spiritual directee, 'Offer your whole soul, a thousand times a day to him.' It is about turning to God, as the sunflower continually turns its face to the sun, to the light which is the source of its life and growth.

One of my great friends, when I was in my 20s and she in her 80s, was Dr Elsie Briggs. She was one of the pioneers of the Julian Groups, which meet for contemplative prayer. Her home is now a retreat centre in Westbury-on-Trym. She was a person of considerable intellect and a voracious reader. Those of us who knew her well would often hear her say to herself (but out loud!), 'Elsie, read less, *ponder* more.' There is something important about letting God speak to our *hearts*. Luke tells us that Mary 'treasured all these words and pondered them in her heart' (2:19).

In what follows, opportunities are given in each chapter to pause and, in that space, first to ponder and then to pray. These times of quiet reflection and giving space to God are intrinsic to the purposes of this book. I am mindful of St Paisios of Athos, who warned those who came to him of the danger of rushing through spiritual books as if this were some kind of accomplishment. He advised rather that it is better to ponder and apply one small sentence of God's word than to read many books about it.

———— ◆ ————

When we give ourselves to God in the measure that he desires, he will know how to bestow us on others, or if he chooses, keep us for himself.
St Basil of Caesarea

John Stroyan

Moses in Front of the Burning Bush (Loca sancta icon)

Remove the sandals from your feet, for the place on which you are standing is holy ground.

EXODUS 3:5

I

Turning aside: to look and to see

Be silent, all people, before the Lord.
ZECHARIAH 2:13

Never be rash with your mouth, nor let your heart be quick to utter a word before God, for God is in heaven, and you upon earth; therefore let your words be few.
ECCLESIASTES 5:2

Silence is a mystery of the age to come, but words are instruments of this world.
St Isaac the Syrian[1]

The first-century writer and bishop, Ignatius of Antioch, wrote, 'It is better to be silent and to be than to make fluent professions and not to be.'[2] These ancient words remind us that there is so much noise, both literally and metaphorically, around us and within us, that we find it hard 'to be silent and to *be*'. We find it hard to 'be still and know' the presence of God (Psalm 46:10). So often we find ourselves caught up in other priorities. Evelyn Underhill, Anglican mystic and teacher, wrote in 1936 that we spend our lives 'conjugating three verbs: to Want, to Have and to Do'. Such desires and activities, she concludes, keep us in 'perpetual unrest; forgetting that none of these verbs have any ultimate significance, except in so far as they are transcended by and included in the fundamental verb to *Be*'.[3]

But what does it mean to *be*? In an age that has rediscovered mindfulness, which actually has ancient Christian roots, it means to be *present*, to be present in the present moment to what *is*. This means, to the Christian, being present to the one who is: that is, to God. In Orthodox iconography, in the icon of Christ, *Pantocrator*, around his face are the words ὁ ὢ ν, 'The one who *is*' (Revelation 1:8). The very name of God, spoken to Moses at the burning bush (Exodus 3), 'I am who I am', means the 'one who is'. So to be present is to be present to the one who is always present to us but to whom we – in our preoccupations – are so rarely present ourselves. In his *Confessions*, Augustine of Hippo put it simply. Addressing God about his early life before he came to faith, he writes, 'You were with me but I was not with you.'[4] In a similar vein, the German Christian mystic Meister Eckhart (1260–1328) writes, 'God is near us, but we are far from him; God is within, we are without; God is at home but we are in a far country.'[5]

God is with us, but so often we are not alert or attentive to his presence.

Being, though, is not simply about being attentive to the presence of God. It is also, by the same token, about being attentive to what is going on around us and within us. It is about living in the present moment or, in the words of the poet R.S. Thomas, 'not hurrying on to a receding future nor hankering after an imagined past'.[6] As the scriptures remind us, it is about the immediacy of 'today' and 'now', as in, for example, the words of the psalmist, later echoed in the letter to the Hebrews, '*Today*, if you hear his voice, do not harden your hearts' (Hebrews 4:7; see Psalm 95:7–8). The apostle Paul also recognises the urgency of an immediate response to the word and presence of God: 'It is *now* the moment for you to wake from sleep' (Romans 13:11); '*Now* is the acceptable time… *now* is the day of salvation' (2 Corinthians 6:2). How often do we prevaricate in our relationship with God? Our minds prefer to engage with the past or the future and resist the present moment. The scriptures, however, make it clear that the time to respond to God is always *now*, *this moment*.

So how alert are we at any given moment to what is going on around us or within us? How attentive are we actually to whatever or whomever is in front of us? What about right now, at this very moment of reading these words? We've all had the experience of reading a page and realising that we haven't taken any of it in! Our minds have been elsewhere; there are so many diverting distractions both within us and around us. The distracting thoughts inside us have been described by the 19th-century Russian saint Theophan the Recluse as like flies buzzing around on a summer's evening.[7] But it is not only the thoughts and voices within us that clamour for and claim our attention; there are also plenty of external distractions. Some of these we *choose* to be distracted by. A wonderful example of a typically contemporary distraction is a Banksy mural in Bristol depicting a young couple. Though embracing each other, the entire attention of each of them is focused on the mobile phone each is holding behind their loved one's head! It epitomises the diffusion of attention that seems to have a grip on most of us.

By way of contrast, an example of concentrated attention can be seen in Stanley Spencer's depiction of a somewhat chubby, bearded but childlike Christ. He is on all fours gazing in rapt attention at some daisies on the ground. It is entitled *Christ in the Wilderness: Consider the lilies*.

Christ in the Wilderness: Consider the lilies (Stanley Spencer)

Have we lost that childlike ability to notice, admire and wonder at God's creation around us? We might ask, with the poet William Davies:

> What is this life if, full of care,
> We have no time to stand and stare?[8]

Vincent van Gogh, whose art was full of extraordinary attentiveness to the glory of God in and through creation, as we see, for example, in his paintings of sunflowers and irises, writes to his brother Theo, 'We must admire more. Most people do not admire enough.'[9]

> I must turn aside and look… and see.
> EXODUS 3:3

Being is also about looking, attending and seeing. Moses turns aside and looks, and sees. He sees a bush aflame with the fire of the glory of God. God tells him to take off his sandals, for the ground on which he is standing is holy. Moses' eyes are opened to see the glory of God in and through God's creation in that particular place (believed to be the site of St Catherine's Monastery in the Sinai desert) and at that particular time. God's words to Moses are particular to him too: 'I am the God of *your* father, the God of Abraham, the God of Isaac, and the God of Jacob' (Exodus 3:6). The universal love of God revealed in and through Abraham, Isaac and Jacob is at the same time for each one of us personally – as particular and unique children of God.

Moreover, the God who meets us personally at a particular time and in a particular place is also the God who is with us at all times and in all places. Holy ground is not simply the ground of God's past encounters with particular people in particular places, the kinds of places to which we go on pilgrimage; it is the ground on which we are actually standing, wherever we are. Poets, inspired by the story of the burning bush, have recognised this. 'Earth's crammed with heaven,' writes Elizabeth Barrett Browning, 'but only he who sees takes off his shoes.'[10] In 'The Bright Field', R.S. Thomas captures something of these moments of transcendence glimpsed in and through God's creation:

> *It is the turning*
> *aside like Moses, to the miracle*
> *of the lit bush, to a brightness*
> *that seemed as transitory as your youth,*
> *once, but is the eternity that awaits you.*[11]

In similar vein, Gerard Manley Hopkins writes, 'The world is charged with the grandeur of God, it will flame out, like shining from shook foil.'[12] As is said or sung in the great prayer of thanksgiving in the Eucharist, 'Heaven and earth are full of your glory.'

When I came back from co-leading a silent retreat in the Sinai desert, my boots were covered in sand. Perhaps childishly, I didn't clean them for some time, reflecting as I did that some of the grains of sand on my boots might have been the actual sand on which Moses stood, barefoot, and that gave me pause for thought. I thought it might be good to hold up one of these boots in a sermon as a prompt to help us to reflect on God's encounter with Moses at the burning bush. In the event, I did hold up one of those boots covered in Sinai sand, but I also held up one of my welly boots, caked in Warwickshire mud. The holy ground of God is the ground on which we stand, whoever we are and wherever we are. Just as we don't have to be or try to be some*one* other than we actually are for God to love us, so we don't have to be some*where* else for God to meet us. On this latter point, Esther de Waal, reflecting on the Benedictine vow of stability, writes, 'The reason for stability? God is not elsewhere.'[13]

The Orthodox daily prayer begins: 'Heavenly king, Comforter, Spirit of truth *who is everywhere and fills all things*… come.' Perhaps even more importantly, the holy ground of God is that which is deep and ineradicably within each of us, made as we are in the image of God. It is where God in his love and grace chooses to come and live. Jesus says, 'Make your home in me just as I do in you' (John 15:4, MSG).

◆

Pause to ponder

When we ponder, we need to slow down. We cannot ponder in a hurry. So we might just want to pause, breathe a bit more deeply and then, prayerfully, to seek what God might be wanting to say to us through the words we are reading or in the silence. It is better to stay with one phrase, sentence or scripture and to spend time on this than to move on quickly in the mistaken belief that the more we get through, the more we will accomplish. In pondering, less is more.

Be still, and know that I am God!
PSALM 46:10

It is impossible for muddy water to grow clear if it is constantly being stirred up.
Neilus of Ankara[14]

The place which Jesus takes in our soul he will never vacate, for in us is his home of homes and it is the greatest delight for him to dwell there.
Mother Julian of Norwich[15]

Pause for prayer

Remember, I am with you always, to the end of the age.
MATTHEW 28:20

Leave the past to the infinite mercy of God, the future to his good providence; give the present wholly to his love.
Jean-Pierre de Caussade[16]

Let us now be still in the presence of God and ask the Holy Spirit to help us to be aware of the presence of God within us and around us.

━━━━━ ◆ ━━━━━

Seeing

Moses turned aside to look and to *see*. Our journey as Christians is a journey into sight. It is a journey into seeing again, seeing more truly, beginning to see as God sees. This journey into seeing begins and continues on earth and is completed in heaven. Paul writes, 'For now we see in a mirror, dimly, but then we will see face to face' (1 Corinthians 13:12). John writes, 'When he is revealed, we will be like him, for we will see him as he is' (1 John 3:2). Disciples – in the New Testament *mathetes* – are by definition learners. Wherever we are on our journey of faith, there is always more for each of us to learn, always more for each of us to see. There is more growing up in Christ for each of us to do (Ephesians 4:15). There is more growing in the knowledge and grace of God for each and all of us to do (2 Peter 3:18). For this learning, for this growing, for this opening of our eyes to happen, we need God's help. We need the Holy Spirit to lead us into the truth (John 16:13). Jesus says to Nicodemus, 'Very truly, I tell you, no one can see the kingdom of God without being born from above' (John 3:3). In other words, we need God's help to see.

The Christian poet and mystic William Blake (1757–1827) writes, 'If the doors of perception were cleansed everything would appear to man as it is, infinite.'[17] Our 'doors of perception', the eyes through which we look, are blinkered. Our sight is – inevitably – partial. This may be because of our unconscious personal or tribal prejudice. It may also be because of what Jesus called 'the beam' in our own eye, which inclines us to see first the sins of others rather than recognising and confessing that within ourselves which prevents us from seeing truly. Without the Holy Spirit, the Spirit of truth, we cannot see our own spiritual blindness.

This means that to begin to see is to begin to see that we do *not* see. Saul, on his way to Damascus to arrest Christians, was clear in his own mind that he was doing God's will. That was how he saw it. At that stage, he couldn't see that he couldn't see. It was not until he was blinded physically by the light of the glory of God that he could begin to see the reality of his own spiritual blindness. Then, when his eyes were opened by the prayer and laying on of hands of Ananias, he could begin to see truly, this time not only physically but also for the first time *spiritually*. Later on, in his correspondence with the fledgling Christian communities he founded, he would contrast the way he used to see, as Saul, which was 'according to the flesh' (*kata sarka*) or 'from a human point of view' (2 Corinthians 5:16), with how he now sees things, which he describes as 'according to the Spirit' (*kata pneuma*) (Romans 8:5). He uses this language of spiritual sight when he prays for the Christians of Ephesus that '*with the eyes of your heart enlightened*, you may know what is the hope to which he has called you' (Ephesians 1:18).

Resisting the truth

Reality check! Do we actually *want* to see? Do we want to allow God to change the way we see things? Do we – if we are honest – actually want to let ourselves 'be transformed by the renewing of [our] minds' (Romans 12:2), to see things differently? Or, like the emperor with his new clothes, have we got too much invested in our comfortable illusions? Are we in fact, however much we might protest to the contrary, like those who say, 'Speak to us smooth things, prophesy illusions' (Isaiah 30:10)? Is our default mode actually to surround ourselves with those who will reinforce in us our own particular ways of seeing things? Is it beyond the bounds of possibility that we, who may seem so enlightened to ourselves, might be like those whom Isaiah (and Jesus in Matthew 13:13) describes as those who are 'ever seeing, but never perceiving' (6:9)? If we hastily reject this even as a possibility, what might *that* be saying about us and our self-awareness?

After all, most of us are dragged kicking and screaming into the truth. T.S. Eliot famously wrote, 'Humankind cannot bear very much reality.'[18] We prefer to see the world, ourselves, others, even God, as we *choose* to see them. We prefer our version of reality to the truth that Jesus promises will set us free (John 8:32). W.H. Auden captures this resistance within us so well:

> *We would rather be ruined than changed*
> *We would rather die in our dread*
> *Than climb the cross of the moment*
> *And let our illusions die.*[19]

But this is what the Holy Spirit does. The Holy Spirit leads us out of our illusions – usually most uncomfortably into the truth. This happens again and again, for example, in the life of the apostle Peter. By the time we meet him in Acts 10, when his worldview is turned upside down once again, he has already had to see many of his illusions die. He had 'known' that the Messiah should never have to suffer and die and had told Jesus as much, before he was fiercely rebuked as 'Satan' for saying so (Matthew 16:22–23). He had 'known' that a rabbi, a teacher, should never wash the feet of his disciples, nor a master those of his slave. So he said to Jesus, 'No, Lord, you must never wash my feet,' only to hear Jesus, his Lord and Master, respond, 'Unless I wash you, you have no share with me' (John 13:8). He had 'known' that he, above all the other apostles, would never deny or disown Jesus and had said to Jesus, 'I will never disown you' (Mark 14:31).

Soon afterwards, having denied knowing Jesus three times, as Jesus had told him he would, we find him weeping bitterly (Luke 22:62). And surely he 'knew' too, at that time of deep contrition, that there could be no question of him, a serial failure as a follower of Christ and one who with James and John slept through Jesus' agony in the garden (Matthew 26:40), becoming leader of the church. But he was met a few days later by the risen Lord, who commissioned him to 'Feed my lambs', 'Tend my sheep', 'Feed my sheep' (John 21:15–17). This is all before he has learnt and seen and witnessed, to his amazement, that 'even the Gentiles' are experiencing the gift of the Holy Spirit. We are called as disciples to be learners and to go on learning. There is always more.

———— ◆ ————

Pause to ponder

To ponder is not so much to think as to *ruminate*. To ruminate, as a cow chews the cud, is to receive more from the food of the words we read. It is to allow the words to go deeper, to speak to our hearts not simply our heads. Benedict begins the Prologue to his *Rule*: 'Listen carefully… and *incline the ears of your heart*.'

> Though I was blind, now I see.
> JOHN 9:25

> It is my belief no man ever understands quite his own artful dodges to escape from the grim shadow of self-knowledge.
> Joseph Conrad[20]

Pause for prayer

Ask the Holy Spirit to help us to see through God's eyes, to enlighten 'the eyes of our hearts' (Ephesians 1:18).

Help us to unlearn what is not of you and to learn what you would teach us. Help us to 'grow up in every way' (Ephesians 4:15).

Forgive us, Lord, if we have stopped believing that we still have much to learn.

Forgive us, Lord, if we are trying to feed on yesterday's manna, not trusting in your fresh manna for today (Exodus 16).

———— ◆ ————

Question: Are there things we can see now, thanks to the Holy Spirit, the Spirit of truth, that we couldn't see before?

———— ◆ ————

Into the desert

> I will charm her, and bring her into the desert, and speak
> tenderly to her heart.
> HOSEA 2:14 (CEB)

> Come apart into a desert place, and rest a little.
> MARK 6:31 (DRA)

> In the deserts of the heart
> let the healing fountain start.
> W.H. Auden[21]

When we look at the scriptures, and also perhaps when we reflect
on our own lives, we will see – though we probably did not at the
time – that it is often the *Spirit of God* who leads us, or drives us, or
simply permits us, to spend time in the desert. That is to say, this is
the desert place where we (re)discover that we cannot 'fix things',
where we cannot in any sense 'save' ourselves. In the economy of
the desert, sooner or later, we discover that our own resources are
not enough. We discover that our sufficiency is not of ourselves and
that, in the words of the apostle Paul, 'our competence is from God'
(2 Corinthians 3:5). In such times, we have to throw ourselves and
our lives on to the mercy of God and God alone. 'But I trust in you,
O Lord; I say, "You are my God." My times are in your hand' (Psalm
31:14–15).

It was the Spirit of God at work in Moses that led the people of
Israel from Egypt through the desert into the promised land. In the
desert, they had to discover and face their own faithlessness and
idolatry. They had to discover that what God wanted for them and
would provide for them if they had faith was so much more for their
blessing than their own plans for their own lives (Deuteronomy
8:2–16; Psalm 106:14–15). In their restless lack of faith, they wanted

to give up and go back, to return to 'the fleshpots of Egypt', rather than trust the promises of God and all that God had for them. Later on in their history, in Hosea, God in his love calls, or woos, his people into the desert to 'speak tenderly to' them (Hosea 2:14).

Jesus of Nazareth, freshly anointed as Christ at his baptism, was immediately *driven* by the Spirit into the wilderness. The Greek word Mark uses, *ekballei*, is one from which we get the word 'ballistic'. The Holy Spirit drives Jesus into this time of testing in the desert, where he was with the wild beasts and angels ministered to him. The desert is where we face up to ultimate realities. It is the Holy Spirit too that leads the freshly anointed Paul, before he sets out on his missionary journeys, into the desert of Arabia (believed to be south of Damascus). He knew he needed time alone with God before engaging with others:

> When God... had set me apart before I was born and called me through his grace... I did not confer with any human being, nor did I go up to Jerusalem to those who were already apostles before me, but I went away at once into Arabia.
> GALATIANS 1:15–17

If we are truly to come to life, the 'life in all its fullness' of which Jesus speaks, the desert, it seems, is an inescapable part of our journey. It is so often in the uncomfortable desert places of our lives that we begin to see again or to see more clearly. The desert is perhaps the one place where we can't escape from ourselves or from God. It is a place where we can't easily hide from the truth as we manage to do in the daily distractions and busyness of our everyday lives. It is a place of reckoning. Far from being a place of escape from the truth, it is a place of facing the truth, of entering more fully into the truth, the truth that sets us free. It is rarely comfortable because, sooner or later, in the desert we must face our own inner poverty, restlessness and aridity and recognise the vacuity of our self-deluding vanities. In short, it is a place where we discover our need of God. But the good news of the gospel is that to be in this place of knowing our need of God is to be in a place of hope and, as Jesus promises, a place of blessing (Matthew 5:3).

Before I co-led a pilgrimage and silent retreat in the Sinai desert, we were warned about the scorpions and snakes we might encounter; we were told to empty our shoes, socks and sleeping bags before we got into them. But many of us were more concerned about the 'snakes and scorpions' we might discover *within us*, as we would be spending so much time in the silence of the desert, away from the occupations and busyness that we allow to distract us from any painful self-revelation. It is here – in the desert, stripped of any illusions of self-sufficiency, in this poverty of spirit – that we know beyond any doubt our utter dependence on the grace and mercy of God. It is here that we can become receptive to the presence of God and a fresh word from God.

The desert also involves *waiting* and perhaps much waiting. One of the things to be handed over altogether is timing: my timing, my expected timing, even my longed-for timing for God to act. In the desert, we discover that the Christian life can never truly be lived with the attitude of 'God on my terms' but only 'God on God's terms'. In the desert, we are reduced to a place of powerlessness, a crucifixion of the egotistical self, where we have no option but to give our lives fully back to God. But the good news of the gospel is that the promise of God is to do precisely what we cannot do without him. We see this in the many prophesies of Isaiah where God promises to make the desert fertile: 'I will make the wilderness a pool of water, and the dry land springs of water' (Isaiah 41:18; see also 32:16; 35:1). God promises to do what is humanly impossible, to do what we could never do for ourselves:

> He split rocks open in the wilderness, and gave them drink abundantly as from the deep. He made streams come out of the rock, and caused waters to flow down like rivers.
> PSALM 78:15–16

In the desert, in God's grace, we may be drawn back to that deep thirst within us that only God can satisfy; and God, who 'thirsts to be thirsted after' (Gregory of Nazianzus), will answer. 'When the poor and needy seek water, and there is none, and their tongue is parched with thirst, I the Lord will answer them' (Isaiah 41:17). So we could say that, for those who truly hunger and thirst for God, there is only one thing worse than having time in the desert and that is *not* having time in the desert.

The desert for most of us, of course, is never going to be a geographical place of scorching sun and sand or in another country. The desert is within us and around us. In our Christian journey, we need neither sand nor sun, nor even a forest (the Russian equivalent), nor even a mountain (the Athonite equivalent). The desert is a translation of the New Testament word *eremos*, from which we get 'hermit'. A hermit in the Christian tradition is one who prays to God, alone. Jesus gets up early to go and pray in 'a desert place' (Mark 1:35, DRA). He calls his disciples away from the noise and demands of the crowd to 'a desert place' (Mark 6:31, DRA). We need time alone with God. The word 'monk' comes from *monos*, which also means 'alone'. We may not be called to be monks, nuns or hermits, but we are all called, every Christian, to have a monastic dimension to our lives.

Time alone with God in 'the desert place' is not only desirable; it is essential. This is foundational to prayer and so also to our relationship with God and his world. Jesus could not make this clearer. 'Whenever you pray, go into your room and shut the door and pray to your Father who is in secret' (Matthew 6:6). Three times in one short sentence, Jesus emphasises that prayer is to be done away from the public eye; and not only away from the *public eye,* but away from *all* eyes, including 'church' eyes. 'Go into your room' – 'shut the door' – 'pray to your Father who is in secret'. Fruitful witness to the love of God in Christ flows from this *hidden* life in Christ: 'you have died, and your life is hidden with Christ in God' (Colossians 3:3). Fruitful witness flows from our life in Christ. Jesus said, 'Those who abide in me and I in them bear much fruit, because apart from me you can do nothing' (John 15:5).

I have heard it said, somewhat mischievously, that the Church of England is like a swimming pool where all the noise is in the shallow end. But the noise will not be shallow if it is a joyful noise and it is offered truly to God. Certainly, the psalms are full of exhortations to be still and to be silent in the presence of God (Psalm 37:7; 46:10; 62:1). Equally, they call us to praise God precisely not *sotto voce* but rather *fortissimo*: 'Make a joyful noise to the Lord, all the earth' (Psalm 98:4; 100:1); 'With trumpets and the sound of the horn, make a joyful noise before the King, the Lord' (Psalm 98:6); 'Praise him with clanging cymbals; praise him with loud clashing cymbals!' (Psalm 150:5). I believe it was Mozart who said, 'The music is not in the notes but in the silence between the notes.' Music needs silence to be what music can be. In the same way, we could say, fruitful participation in the mission of God flows from time with God 'in the desert place'. Elijah hears the word of God not in the wind, earthquake or fire but in the 'sound of sheer silence' (1 Kings 19:12). God's word for us and God's word through us come from our time in the silence of God.

◆

Pause to ponder

To ponder is not so much about thinking with our heads but receiving in our hearts. To ponder the word of God in the scriptures is a profound form of prayer in which we allow God to speak to us, to feed us from within and so to bring us to life, to inspire us and to equip us. We are invited by the apostle Paul to 'let the word of Christ dwell in you richly' (Colossians 3:16). Jesus says, 'If you abide in me, and my words abide in you, ask for whatever you wish, and it will be done for you' (John 15:7).

Be silent, all people, before the Lord; for he has roused himself
from his holy dwelling.
ZECHARIAH 2:13

We shall never be safe in the market place unless we are at
home in the desert.
Cardinal Basil Hume[22]

All the troubles of life come upon us because we refuse to sit
quietly for a whole hour each day in our rooms.
Blaise Pascal[23]

St Anne (Bose Monastery)

Pause for prayer

For God alone my soul waits in silence.
PSALM 62:1

Drop thy still dews of quietness,
till all our strivings cease;
Take from our souls the strain and stress,
and let our ordered lives confess
the beauty of thy peace.[24]

Teach us, Lord God, to silence our voices and to still our minds that we may hear in our hearts the whisper of your Holy Spirit within us, in the sound of sheer silence.

———— ◆ ————

Jesus' question to us: 'And can any of you by worrying add a single hour to your span of life?' (Matthew 6:27).

The Return (Solomon Raj)

But while he was still far off, his father saw him and was filled with compassion; he ran and put his arms around him and kissed him.

LUKE 15:20

2

Turning to Christ: repentance

Repentance and mercy

Blessed are the merciful, for they will receive mercy.
MATTHEW 5:7

Remember this and you will no longer judge. Judas was an apostle and the thief crucified at Christ's right hand was a murderer. What a transformation in an instant!
St John Climacus[1]

While the church has often been perceived and indeed experienced as more judgemental than merciful, what was most scandalous about Jesus – especially to the religious – was not his condemnation but his mercy. Indeed, his anger was directed most of all at those who were seemingly oblivious to their own profound need of God's mercy, and who stood in self-righteous judgement of others.

Many years ago, I was in a production of the Victorian melodrama *Sweeney Todd*. I played the villain, Todd. In Victorian melodrama, as in contemporary pantomime, the tradition is to hiss or boo the villain when he or she comes on and to cheer the hero or heroine. We toured the production around many venues where I, as Todd, was duly hissed and the hero duly cheered. The last venue we played in was Perth Prison. It turned out differently there. When I came on stage, I was cheered. When the hero came on stage, he was booed. But the loudest boo by far was when the judge came on!

But, of course, the world doesn't divide between 'goodies' and 'baddies'. The great Russian writer Aleksandr Solzhenitsyn was sent to a labour camp for his outspoken criticism of the corruption of communism in the Soviet Union. He was lionised by the west for his prophetic and trenchant critique, and was expelled from the Soviet Union in 1974. When he experienced life in America, he challenged the spiritual vacuity and materialism of western culture. Many in North America who had applauded his critique of communism resented his criticism of capitalist consumerism. Solzhenitsyn wouldn't collude with the mutual demonisation going on between east and west or, for that matter, between any ideologies. He wrote: 'Gradually it was disclosed to me that the line separating good and evil passes not through states, nor between classes, nor between political parties either – but right through every human heart.'[2] Demonising or judging others reinforces our self-righteousness and allows us not to face, not to recognise, what Jesus called 'the log' in our own eye (Matthew 7:5). Our judging of others both derives from spiritual blindness and in turn compounds it. Mother Julian of Norwich wrote:

> Looking at another's sin clouds the eyes of the soul, unless we look upon this sinner with contrition with him, compassion on him, and a holy longing to God for him. Otherwise it must harm and disquiet and hinder the soul that looks upon these sins.[3]

When Simone Weil joined the Republican fight in the Spanish Civil War, she was shocked at the degree of violence she witnessed perpetrated by one human being against another. She was even more shocked when she recognised that:

> I have the germ of all possible crimes, or nearly all within me. I felt the possibility of them within myself. It was actually because I felt this possibility in myself that they filled me with such horror.[4]

Those rushing to stone to death the woman caught in adultery, as recorded in John 8, are stopped in their tracks by the words of Jesus: 'Let anyone among you who is without sin be the first to throw a stone at her' (v. 7). Tellingly, it is the oldest among her accusers, presumably those with a greater degree of self-knowledge, who are the first to walk away. It is to this self-awareness that Isabella, in Shakespeare's *Measure for Measure*, appeals when she pleads to Angelo for the life of her brother, Claudio.

> How would you be
> if he who is the top of judgement should
> but judge you as you are?
> O think on that
> and mercy then will breathe upon your lips
> like man made new.[5]

Jesus says, 'For with the judgement you make you will be judged, and the measure you give will be the measure you get' (Matthew 7:2). So it is that John Chrysostom can say, 'The judgement on us depends on us'.[6] The world does not divide between those who need God and those who do not. It divides, surely, between those who *know* their need of God and those who do not.

——— ◆ ———

Pause to ponder

> Be merciful, just as your Father is merciful.
> LUKE 6:36

> Our sins against God are immeasurably greater than others' sins against us.
> St Isaac the Syrian[7]

> Don't call God just – his justice is not manifested to you, your many sins have been overlooked.
> St Isaac the Syrian[8]

Pause for prayer

God, be merciful to me, a sinner!
LUKE 18:13

O Lord and Master of my life, take from me the spirit of sloth, despair, lust of power and idle talk. But give me rather the spirit of chastity, humility, patience and love. Yea, O Lord and King, grant me to see my own transgressions and not judge my brother or sister, for blessed art thou, unto the ages of ages. Amen
Traditional prayer of St Ephrem

———— ◆ ————

The good news of repentance

There will be more joy in heaven over one sinner who repents than over ninety-nine righteous people who need no repentance.
LUKE 15:7

Return to me, and I will return to you, says the Lord of hosts.
MALACHI 3:7

When I was a parish priest, a woman who didn't go to church came up to me in the street and, referring to a member of the congregation, said, 'So and so goes to church, but I know what she's really like.' I said to her something like, 'If you came to church – and you would be most welcome – you would hear all of us recognising before one another and God that we have messed up, we have fallen short; in traditional language, we have sinned. We need God's forgiveness.' The Christian is one who knows he or she is not good and who knows he or she needs God's mercy. If this were not the case, we would be perjuring ourselves every time we say or pray the confession!

However unfashionable the idea of repentance may be in today's world, turning to God, turning to Christ, is not simply desirable; it is essential in the Christian life. There is and can be no Christian life without repentance, without *metanoia*, without some real change of mind and change of direction. The Old Testament prophets, again and again, call the erring and idolatrous people of God to repent and return to the Lord (Hosea 6:1; Joel 2:13; Isaiah 30:15; Ezekiel 18:30–32). The gospel begins with a call to repentance. John the Baptist heralds the coming of the Messiah with the words 'Repent, for the kingdom of heaven has come near' (Matthew 3:2). Jesus, freshly anointed at his baptism, proclaims, 'The time is fulfilled, and the kingdom of God has come near; repent, and believe in the good news' (Mark 1:15).

Repentance is a response to the kingdom, to new creation, to the Holy Spirit who makes all things new. It is not about old-order living. It is not about improving our lives in the old order. We often, in our thinking, get this wrong. Repentance is not simply about being or saying 'sorry' to God and hoping to get better at living in the old order. Repentance is a response to the new life of Christ, to the breaking in of the kingdom of God. George MacDonald described three stages of the Christian journey: the old person in the old order; the new person in the old order; the new person in the new order. True repentance is a response to the amazing grace of God, to the breaking in of the new life of the kingdom. In Acts 2, when the crowds from all over the world gather in Jerusalem at Pentecost, they witness the power and presence of the Holy Spirit moving among the disciples and ask, 'What should we do?' Peter responds, 'Repent, and be baptised every one of you in the name of Jesus Christ so that your sins may be forgiven; and you will receive the gift of the Holy Spirit' (Acts 2:37–38).

Jesus announces, 'I have come to call not the righteous but sinners to repentance' (Luke 5:32). The risen Lord, opening the minds of the disciples to understand the scriptures, says to them, 'Thus it is written, that the Messiah is to suffer and to rise from the dead on the third day, and that repentance and forgiveness of sins is to be proclaimed in his name to all nations' (Luke 24:46–47). Repentance and forgiveness are not simply aspects of the gospel proclamation; they are the core content (the *kerygma*). The Holy Spirit is given to witness to this gospel. Later, Paul exhorts the Athenians at the Areopagus to repent: 'Now he commands all people everywhere to repent, because he has fixed a day on which he will have the world judged' (Acts 17:30–31). Likewise, when in Luke's moving account Paul bids farewell to the Ephesian elders, he encapsulates the core message he has communicated in Ephesus: 'I testified to both Jews and Greeks about repentance towards God and faith towards our Lord Jesus' (Acts 20:21).

So it is that John Wesley, who experienced profoundly the joy of sins forgiven some twelve years after his ordination, could write, 'Repentance is the porch to religion, faith is the door and holiness is the essence of religion.'[9] Liturgical prayer, in both eastern and western traditions, is steeped in both the call to repentance and in the response of public corporate confession.

Dimensions of repentance

But what is repentance? Among *The Homilies*, which were required to be read out in churches across the Church of England in the second half of the 16th century, Homily 19 was entitled 'An Homilie of Repentance and True Reconciliation unto God'. Urging 'a speedy returning unto the Lord God of Hostes', it identifies four dimensions of repentance, each drawn from the scriptures. The first is 'contrition of the heart' (Psalm 51:17). The second is 'an unfeigned confession and acknowledging our sins before God' (Psalm 32:5; 1 John 1:9; James 5:16). The third is faith 'where we apprehend and take hold of God's promises of pardon and forgiveness' (Luke 5:32; 1 Timothy 1:15; 1 John 1:9). The fourth is 'an amendment of life, or a new life, which demonstrates the fruits of repentance' (Matthew 3:8).[10]

True repentance, then, both embraces and transcends liturgical and sacramental confession. To confess our sins personally and corporately is an indispensable part of spiritual health. It is indeed, as the adage goes, 'good for the soul'. But repentance is something deeper and wider than this. It both precedes true confession and is released afresh following the experience of forgiveness. It is more than simply the 'event' of personal or corporate confession and the receiving of absolution. Repentance includes a deeper movement of the heart in response to God's love. In fact, it would be as true to say that repentance *follows* forgiveness, as it would be to say that forgiveness follows repentance. Benedict in the Prologue to his *Rule* quotes Paul, 'Do you not realise that God's kindness is meant to lead you to repentance?' (Romans 2:4). Repentance is a response to the love and the kindness of God. Both as a parish priest and in my time since, I have been privileged to experience and to witness deep tears of repentance, tears that have flowed through the apprehension of God's forgiveness and deep love for us. It is the love of God that moves us to true repentance more than the judgement of God.

When the prodigal son 'came to himself', in Luke's memorable phrase (Luke 15:17), he turns. He has recognised the gravity of what he has done and he turns back home to his father in penitence. This is before he experiences his father's forgiveness. But the experience of his father's unconditional and lavishly generous welcome back, one imagines, releases within him a deeply joyful repentance, a repentance which flows this time not from guilt but rather from the joyful experience of his father's unconditional love and forgiveness: a new movement of love for his father, a love responding to his father's love, a love that he had never experienced before leaving home. So we might want to say two things: first that repentance leads to joy, and second that repentance – a turning in love to Christ – flows from joy, the joy of being forgiven.

Repentance and joy

> Repentance is the daughter of hope and the renunciation of despair.
>
> St John Climacus[11]

> Repentance is given to humanity as grace after grace, for repentance is a second regeneration by God.
>
> St Isaac the Syrian[12]

So repentance is not, as some still imagine it to be, some gloomy duty to suppress our spirits or to make sure miserable sinners remain miserable. On the contrary, it is what the Orthodox call 'joy-giving'. It brings joy in heaven (Luke 15:7) and on earth (Psalm 32:1). We might think of the overflowing of joy in John Wesley when he felt his heart 'strangely warmed' and – his diary continues – 'I felt I did trust in Christ, Christ alone for salvation, and an assurance was given me that he had taken away my sins, even mine, and saved me from the law of sin and death.'[13] This experience of forgiveness released in him the extraordinary energies of the Holy Spirit to witness to the gospel of the forgiveness of sins, so that many thousands of lives were transformed through the transformation of his life. The repentance that leads to joy and indeed flows from joy, however, comes not from avoiding but from facing our need for the grace and mercy of God. Before going, on 24 May 1738, 'very unwillingly' to this meeting at Aldersgate Street which was to change his life, Wesley had had to face his own spiritual poverty and the ineffectiveness of his own Christian witness. On returning from his mission to America, he wrote, 'I went to America to convert the Indians, but who shall convert me? I have a fair summer religion. I can talk well but let death look me in the face and my spirit is troubled.'[14] Wesley had to face his own inner aridity, he had to enter 'the desert place' of seeing and facing his own insufficiency, before he was ready to experience the joy and release of forgiveness and an anointing for ministry and mission.

Joy and penitence go hand in hand. They belong together. Jesus blesses those who know their need of God and of his mercy. If, however, we focus simply on our frailty and falling short and lose sight of God's mercy, the result will be despondency. If, on the other hand, we take God's mercy for granted and lose sight of our continuing need for it, the result is likely to be a subtle spiritual complacency or even triumphalism. Macarius, a fourth-century Egyptian saint, of whom Wesley wrote in his diary, 'he made my heart sing',[15] warns of those who 'having received the grace of the Spirit begin to rely on this fact and become puffed up. They forget the need for a broken heart and humility of spirit.'[16] Richard Hooker writes of a 'happy mixture' of a sense of our own unworthiness and a trust in the mercy of God through Jesus.[17] Similarly, Mother Julian of Norwich describes 'the marvellous medley of wellbeing and unease in which we have in us our Lord Jesus Christ uprising and we have in us the wretchedness and misery of Adam falling'.[18] Both are necessary. In his *Journal of a Soul*, Pope John XXIII quotes words, attributed to Pope Innocent III, which capture this bifocal necessity in Christian life. He writes of:

> … the humble prayer of a Christian who thinks of sin but is aware of forgiveness, who thinks of death but with a heart that is sure of the resurrection, who knows the magnitude of his own unworthiness but knows even better the greater magnitude of the Lord's mercy.[19]

Just as faith and repentance cannot be separated, so too joy and penitence belong together. They are, in the words of the Anglican theologian Henry Bull (1530–77), 'knit as companions together, albeit the one driveth us down with fear and the other lifteth us up with comfort, so in prayer they must needs meet together'.[20] This knitting together of joy and penitence is, of course, epitomised in the Jesus Prayer of the Orthodox Church. It begins with an affirmation of faith in the Lordship of Jesus as God – 'Lord Jesus Christ…' – and continues with the recognition of our deep need of God's mercy each moment – '… have mercy on me, a sinner.' (The Lord's Prayer likewise begins with the hallowing of the name of God before the acknowledging of our dependence on God's provision and mercy.) Turning to Christ flows from the Spirit of truth at work within us, the Spirit that convinces us that 'if we say that we have no sin, we deceive ourselves, and the truth is not in us' (1 John 1:8). Isaac the Syrian writes:

> When a sinner becomes aware of his failings and begins to repent, he is already righteous; when a righteous man becomes aware of his righteousness and his conscience is persuaded of it, he is already a sinner.[21]

The parable of the Pharisee and tax collector exemplifies this, reminding us that it is in the place of penitent humility that we are justified before God (Luke 18:14). A broken and contrite heart God will not despise (Psalm 51:17). Charles Simeon (1759–1836), who had a profound and converting experience of Christ when receiving Holy Communion, was vicar of Holy Trinity, Cambridge for many years. Many thousands were converted through his ministry. At the heart of his profoundly evangelical faith, Simeon longed to be in this place of contrition, or 'dust', at all times, the 'only safe place for a Christian':

> The tender heart, the broken and contrite spirit are to me far above all the joys that I could hope for in this vale of tears. I long to be in my proper place, my hand on my mouth and my mouth in the dust. I feel this is safe ground. Here I cannot err.[22]

So Simeon speaks of 'the happy condition of the self-condemning penitent'. This penitence, as we have seen, is so much more than the discrete events of confession – vital though they are. It is a condition, a way of being, that attracts the grace of God. Simeon knew that the place where God works in us and flows through us most freely is the place of penitent humility. As the poet Henry Vaughan puts it:

> *And here, in dust and dirt – oh, here,*
> *The lilies of his love appear!*[23]

———— ◆ ————

Pause to ponder

The sacrifice acceptable to God is a broken spirit; a broken and contrite heart, O God, you will not despise.
PSALM 51:17

If there be anywhere on earth a lover of God who is always kept safe from falling, I know nothing of it – for it was not shown me. But this was shown: that in falling and rising again we are always held close in one love.
Mother Julian of Norwich[24]

I believe, too, often our Lord deliberately chooses to work in those who have been habitual sinners rather than in those who by comparison have never grieved him at all.
The Cloud of Unknowing[25]

Pause for prayer

If we say that we have no sin, we deceive ourselves, and the truth is not in us.
1 JOHN 1:8

Lord, help us to see ourselves truly in the light of your love. Show us as much as we can bear to see to bring us to true repentance and to taste the joy of forgiveness.

———— ◆ ————

Repentance and sight

Now my eye sees you; therefore I despise myself, and repent in
dust and ashes.
JOB 42:5–6

The more progress we make in the spiritual life, the more we
see our need for repentance.
St Paisios of Mount Athos[26]

O wad some Power the giftie gie us.
To see oursels as ithers see us!
It wad frae monie a blunder free us
An' foolish notion.
Robert Burns[27]

Many years ago, I spent some time down a coal mine in Yorkshire
as part of an Industrial Mission course. Having spent several hours
underground in considerable darkness, I remember coming up in
the cage and being dazzled by the daylight. It was not until my eyes
had become accustomed to the light that I could see how covered
in grime and coal dust I and the others were. I couldn't see this in
the darkness. Karl Barth wrote that we can only see the extent of
the problem when we have been grasped by the solution. We need
the light of Christ to see truly. As the psalmist writes, 'With you is the
fountain of life; in your light we see light' (Psalm 36:9).

The Christian journey, as described by Athonite Father Aimilianos,
is one in which we are led by the Holy Spirit 'to see ourselves as we
truly are in the light of the glory of God'.[28] Seeing ourselves in the light
of the glory of God cannot but lead to repentance. So Dorotheus of
Gaza writes, 'So also the saints, the nearer they get to God, the more
they see themselves as sinners.'[29] When Isaiah encounters the light
of the glory of God in the temple, he sees the stark reality of his own
sinfulness and that of God's people: 'Woe is me! I am lost, for I am a
man of unclean lips, and I live among a people of unclean lips; yet my

eyes have seen the King, the Lord of hosts!' (Isaiah 6:5). He needs to see his own frailty and fallenness before he is ready to be forgiven, cleansed, anointed and sent. When Job finally *sees* God, having heard so much and argued so much about God with his 'comforters', he cannot but repent: 'I had heard of you by the hearing of the ear, but now my eye sees you; therefore I despise myself, and repent in dust and ashes' (Job 42:5–6). Although our journey is a journey into sight, God in his mercy does not reveal to us more than we can bear. The good news of the gospel is that God works in and through frail earthen vessels. The treasures of the kingdom are given to and through pots of clay. Our weaknesses, our fallibilities, far from being an obstacle to God's life and work in and through us, are, if acknowledged before God, the very raw material of his transforming grace.

The gift of limitation

So, I will boast all the more gladly of my weaknesses, so that the power of Christ may dwell in me. Therefore I am content with weaknesses, insults, hardships, persecutions, and calamities for the sake of Christ; for whenever I am weak, then I am strong.
2 CORINTHIANS 12:9–10

Rejoice every time you discover a new imperfection.
Jean-Pierre De Caussade[30]

Do not be disheartened by our imperfections. Our very perfection lies in diligently contending against them.
Francis de Sales[31]

Liberty is bound up with imperfection, and limitations and imperfections. Errors are not only unavoidable but salutary.
Thomas Merton[32]

Human frailty is part of the divine economy that leads us to see our need of God and so prepares us to receive his mercy and grace. As

Mother Julian of Norwich wrote in 1373, during a severe illness in which she received her 'shewings' or *Revelations of Divine Love*:

> We need to fall and to see that we have fallen. For if we never fell we should not know how weak and pitiable we are in ourselves. Nor should we know the wonderful love of our maker.[33]

To know, to recognise, to discover our insufficiency, our lack, our need, is a gift. It is a gift because it awakens our longings and our desire not only for forgiveness, for healing, for strength and for guidance, but also for God himself, who has placed these longings within us. To be hungry for God, to be thirsty for God, is a sure sign of the presence of God within us. So Anselm prays: 'O Lord, give me what you have made me want… and grant me what you have made me long for.'[34] It is the Spirit of God at work in us that evokes our hunger for God. God in us draws us back to God. Thomas Traherne, Anglican priest and poet (1637–74), writes about this 'want' as a gift of God. For Traherne, 'want' embraces two meanings: 'lack' and 'desire'. So, this 'want' is a true gift of God: 'From eternity it was requisite that we should want, our own wants are treasures.' He goes on, 'Be present with your want of a Deity and you shall be present with the Deity.'[35] Our deepest longings come from God and lead us back to God. As Augustine of Hippo famously prays, 'O God, you have made us for yourself and our hearts are restless, till they find their rest in you.'[36]

It is important, however, not only to know with Paul our own insufficiency without God (2 Corinthians 3:5), but also to recognise this with one another and before God, to know that we are beggars together before God. The Puritan Richard Baxter writes in *The Reformed Pastor* words not only for all clergy but also surely for all Christians:

> Our whole work must be carried on in a sense of our own insufficiency and in a pious, believing dependence upon Christ. Ministers have need of one another; and the self-sufficient are the most deficient and commonly proud and empty men.[37]

It is so often when facing and sharing our weakness and insufficiency before God, and then in our reaching out together to God, that God chooses to act. Stephen Verney's *Fire in Coventry* tells the story of an extraordinary spiritual renewal in the Coventry Diocese which began with clergy letting go of any competitive spirit and sharing together their real struggles and failures. This facing of the truth in mutual vulnerability and humility gave space for God to act. It is to this corporate dimension of Christian life that we now turn in the next chapter.

———— ◆ ————

Pause to ponder

As a deer longs for flowing streams, so my soul longs for you, O God.

PSALM 42:1

God thirsts to be thirsted after.

St Gregory of Nazianzus[38]

Anyone who wholeheartedly desires God already possesses him whom he loves, for no one would be able to love God if he did not possess him whom he loves.

St Gregory[39]

Pause for prayer

O Lord, all my longing is known to you; my sighing is not hidden from you.

PSALM 38:9

O God, you are my God, I seek you, my soul thirsts for you.

PSALM 63:1

Let us be present before God with our longings and know his presence with us.

We might want to make our own the prayer of Anselm:

> Give me what you have made me want… and grant me what you have made me long for.[40]

———— ◆ ————

Jesus' question to us: 'Why do you see the speck in your neighbour's eye, but do not notice the log in your own eye?' (Matthew 7:3).

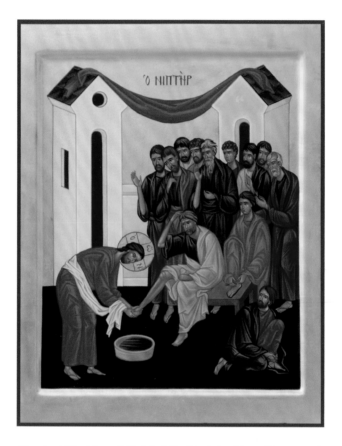

The Foot-Washing of Christ of the Disciples (Bose Monastery)

Just as I have loved you, you also should love one another.
JOHN 13:34

3

Turning in love: for one another

When brothers and sisters live together in unity

How very good and pleasant it is, when kindred live together in unity!
PSALM 133:1

By this everyone will know that you are my disciples, if you have love for one another.
JOHN 13:35

We know that we have passed from death to life because we love one another.
1 JOHN 3:14

I remember hearing about a vicar who, presumably after preaching a sermon on reconciliation, said to the members of the congregation, 'Today, when you share the peace, I would encourage you first of all to go to someone you don't like at all and exchange the peace with them.' Though the advice was well intentioned, you can imagine the result. They all froze! When Tertullian wrote, 'See how these Christians love one another,'[1] he meant it. This at least was how he imagined pagans would respond to the evident love of Christians for God and one another, witnessed not least in their martyrdom, when they would often be seen exchanging the peace just before they were killed. Tertullian could see the missional power of Christian martyrdom, claiming that 'the blood of the martyrs is the seed of the church'.[2] Sadly, today when his words about Christians so evidently loving one another are quoted, it is usually with irony or cynicism in the context of Christian relationships which reveal little or no love.

A retired bishop I know was visiting Mother Teresa of Calcutta. At that stage, he was involved in the training of missionaries. Just before he left, he asked her, 'What is the most important thing I should tell them?' She answered simply, 'Tell them to love one another.' Teresa of Ávila writes, 'What value God places on our loving and keeping peace with one another! The good Jesus places it before anything else.'[3] Whether we like it or not, we cannot escape the fact that, in Marshall McLuhan's famous phrase from the 1960s, 'the medium is the message'. It is the quality of our relationships with one another, with God and with God's world that will communicate the reality – or otherwise – of the love of Christ in us. More recently, Lesslie Newbigin, whose life and writings communicated so much of the presence and reality of God, wrote that 'the church is the hermeneutic of the gospel'. He argued that for the gospel to be credible, 'it is necessary to have a congregation of men and women who believe it and *live* by it'.[4]

We see in Jesus' high priestly prayer that both the credibility and the consequent fruitfulness of our witness are directly related to the love we have and are *seen* to have for one another. If we do not have this love for one another, we fail and fall at the first hurdle. Jesus prays, 'As you, Father, are in me and I am in you, may they also be in us, *so that the world may believe* that you have sent me.' He continues to pray, 'that they may become completely one, *so that the world may know* that you have sent me' (John 17:21, 23). If we believe that every human being is made in the image of God, it should come as no surprise that there is an instinctive or intuitive recognition of the presence – or absence – of the love of God at work in Christian lives and communities. People, of whatever faith or none, can see with John, that 'those who say, "I love God", and hate their brothers or sisters, are liars' (1 John 4:20).

But what are some of the constituent ingredients of this love for one another? What makes for Christian unity? The simplest answer is Christ. Christian unity begins, continues and finds fulfilment only in Christ and through Christ. It cannot be achieved or manipulated simply by human effort, skill or diplomacy. That is to say, it is a gift of God. To grow into this unity, our focus needs to be not on each other but on God. Dorotheus of Gaza, a sixth-century monk in Palestine, stresses this. He invites us to imagine that the world is a circle with God as the centre. The radii are the different ways human beings live. When those who seek to come closer to God move towards the centre, they come closer to all others who are seeking God first.[5] Unity in Christ is based on relationship with Christ and can never be discovered independently of this.

If we are serious about Christian unity, it will not be sufficient, no matter how worthy our motives, to seek it simply on the 'horizontal' plane, looking across at one another and seeking commonalities across our differences. The 'vertical' dimension is essential, indeed primary, in this quest. As the psalmist writes, 'Unless the Lord builds the house, those who build it labour in vain' (Psalm 127:1). Christian unity cannot be achieved simply by creative ecumenical engineering, however important this may sometimes be. It is a gift of God, enabled by the Holy Spirit, the Spirit of truth. Integral to Jesus' prayer for unity is his prayer that we may be sanctified 'in the truth; your word is truth' (John 17:17). So the building blocks of this unity have to include prayer and holiness. Michael Ramsey pulled no punches when he said:

> What is wrong with Christendom is not only that we are divided, it is also that we lack holiness and that we monkey about with the truth. That being so, it seems to me entirely insufficient to think and talk about reunion unless in the same breath we are thinking and talking about re-consecration and recovery of the fullness of truth.[6]

Some words from the letter to the Hebrews are pertinent here. 'Pursue peace with everyone, and the holiness without which no one will see the Lord' (Hebrews 12:14). So what are some of the signs of the Spirit of God, the Spirit of unity, being alive in the Christian community?

Forgiveness

> Be kind to one another, tender-hearted, forgiving one another,
> as God in Christ has forgiven you.
> EPHESIANS 4:32

> To refuse to forgive is to betray our humanity.
> St Maximus Confessor[7]

The story is told of a very public sinner who was excommunicated and forbidden entry to the church. He took his woes to God: 'They won't let me in because I'm a sinner.' 'What are you complaining about?' said God. 'They won't let me in either!'

As we have seen, the unity into which we are called is a unity of sinners, forgiven and forgiving. The church is emphatically not, as Dietrich Bonhoeffer stressed, a community of 'the pious'.[8] Nor is it a community of 'good' people, least of all those who think they are good. As Thomas Merton put it, 'A saint is not a good person but one who has experienced the goodness of God.'[9] It is a community of people united in the knowledge both of their need of God and their experience of the mercy of God. It is a community of people who have experienced something new, a new dimension to life has opened up. Aristides (second century) describes Christians as 'a new people with something divine in the midst of them'.[10]

An ordained friend of mine told me that the nearest he had come to *koinonia*, or 'the fellowship of the Holy Spirit', as he understood it, was when he was invited to attend a meeting of Alcoholics Anonymous. There, he witnessed real mutual confession (James 5:16), a profound sense of solidarity and mutual support (1 Thessalonians 5:11) and, of course, a common recognition of the need of a higher power, of God (Jeremiah 17:14). Our unity is the unity of the forgiven and forgiving, as recognised in the Lord's Prayer, 'Forgive us our sins as we forgive those who sin against us.' 'To refuse to forgive,' wrote Maximus Confessor, 'is to betray our humanity.'[11]

This is because the truth about humanity, about every one of us, is that we need both to be forgiven and to forgive. We need God's mercy and, recognising this truth about ourselves and all our sisters and brothers, we need also to be merciful. The merciful receive God's mercy. Communities of mercy reveal the victory of Christ, who on the cross prayed, 'Father, forgive them, for they know not what they do' (Luke 22:34). Dorotheus of Gaza, referring to the palm and olive branches used to herald and celebrate Christ as Messiah as he entered Jerusalem on a donkey, writes, 'The palm-branch is the symbol of the victory [of Christ in which Christians share]. The olive branch is the symbol of mercy.'[12] Christ's victory is revealed in and through communities of mercy; in short, when you and I and we are merciful. Christ's victory is revealed not through our domination of others, nor through our judging of others, but through mercy and forgiveness. This is what makes a new start possible.

Forgiveness releases not only the one(s) forgiven; it releases also the one(s) forgiving. In Leo Tolstoy's *Anna Karenina* (1877), Anna's husband, Alexei, betrayed by Anna's affair with Vronsky, after much pain and embitterment is given – unexpectedly to himself and to the reader – grace to forgive both Anna and Vronsky. Through this forgiveness he is profoundly changed. Tolstoy writes of Alexei:

> He suddenly felt that the very thing that had once been the source of his suffering had become the source of his spiritual joy, that what had seemed insoluble when he condemned, reproached and hated became simple and clear when he forgave and loved.[13]

Through forgiving, through the mercy that we demonstrate to others, we ourselves are released in God's mercy into a new freedom. Real life, of course, teaches us that this is not easy. We need God's help.

———— ◆ ————

Pause to ponder

Forgive us our debts, as we also have forgiven our debtors.
MATTHEW 6:12

Let a merciful heart preside over your entire way of life and you will be at peace with God.
St Isaac the Syrian[14]

Offer to him your heart, soft and pliable... lest you lose the imprint of his fingers.
St Irenaeus of Lyons[15]

Pause for prayer

If we confess our sins, he who is faithful and just will forgive us our sins and cleanse us from all unrighteousness.
1 JOHN 1:9

If our hearts have become hardened through not asking for forgiveness or not forgiving others, let us pray for the softening of our hearts. Invite the Holy Spirit, who brings to light things hidden in darkness, gently to reveal to us where we need to receive forgiveness and where we need to forgive.

————— ◆ —————

Praise and thanksgiving

As Christians, we are united not only in our common need to be forgiven and to forgive. We are united also as a people of praise and thanksgiving. As the psalmist writes, 'Let the peoples praise you, O God; let all the peoples praise you' (Psalm 67:5).

From the rising of the sun to its setting the name of the Lord is
to be praised.
PSALM 113:3

Praise the Lord! Praise the Lord, O my soul! I will praise the Lord
as long as I live.
PSALM 146:1-2

Yet you are holy, enthroned on the praises of Israel.
PSALM 22:3

Our chief end, the Westminster Catechism reminds us, is to worship
God and enjoy him forever. Every time we gather around the Lord's
table, we remind ourselves that it is our duty and our joy at all times
and in all places to give God thanks and praise. To say that it is our
'duty' is to speak of the *discipline* of praise or even, as the writer to
the Hebrews puts it, the '*sacrifice* of praise' (Hebrews 13:15). The
apostle Paul bids his readers to give thanks '*in* all circumstances'
(1 Thessalonians 5:18). We are called also to give thanks '*for*
everything' (Ephesians 5:20). There is a danger, perhaps especially in
the west, of becoming 'consumers' in our approach to God: to praise
God only when we feel like it or when we think we have a particular
thing to thank him for. Father Benson SSJE, however, insists on a
strong biblical foundation: 'We do not praise God because he has
caused us to triumph, but because to praise God is to triumph.'[16]

Praise and thanksgiving, then, are not to be conditional or dependent
on the circumstances around us or within us, or on whether we
deem them to be worthy of praise and thanksgiving. Paul, writing
from prison, invites his readers to 'rejoice in the Lord always; again
I will say, Rejoice' (Philippians 4:4). Paul and Silas, in the stocks in
prison in Philippi, still smarting from the wounds of their flogging,
sing praises to God (Acts 16:25–34). I think of Jacob Kwashi, the
then Dean of Kaduna, Nigeria, who shared with some others and
me an account of a church being burnt down by so-called Muslims
(here we need to recognise that there was also reciprocal violence

by so-called Christians). The following morning, a large crowd of Christians gathered around the smouldering remains of the church, not to lament or to harbour thoughts of revenge but to praise God. This apparently confounded the perpetrators and other witnesses, who could not believe such a reaction to such a malicious action.

If God is 'enthroned on the praises of Israel' (Psalm 22:3) or, as other translations have it, '*inhabits* the praises of his people', then this worship changes us. Praise changes the ecology within us. To worship God in Spirit and in truth is to give God space to change us. Praise and thanksgiving to a Christian can never be optional. They are foundational to staying alive in Christ. They are, as our liturgy reminds us, 'our duty and our joy'. Without the discipline or duty of praise – that is to say, praising God, whether we feel like it or not – it is unlikely we will discover that this duty is also a joy. When we praise, when we worship God in Spirit and in truth, we make space for God's renewing and healing work within us.

As we are changed by praise, so the circumstances in which we find ourselves are changed. Why? Because we are part of those circumstances.

———— ◆ ————

Pause to ponder

Through [Jesus], then, let us continually offer a sacrifice of praise to God, that is, the fruit of lips that confess his name.
HEBREWS 13:15

Seven whole days, not one in seven, I will praise thee.
George Herbert[17]

Lift up your heart to God with humble love: and mean God himself, and not what you get out of him.
The Cloud of Unknowing[18]

Pause for prayer

Bless the Lord, O my soul, and all that is within me, bless his holy name.
PSALM 103:1

Rejoice always, pray without ceasing, give thanks in all circumstances.
1 THESSALONIANS 5:16–18

Let us pray for both the desire and the discipline to give thanks and praise to God at all times and in all places.

Thou that hast given so much to me,
Give one thing more, a grateful heart…
Not thankful, when it pleaseth me;
As if thy blessings had spare days:
But such a heart, whose pulse may be
Thy praise.
George Herbert[19]

Spend time in praise of God, and for who God is, not for what we can get out of him.

———— ◆ ————

Getting out of the way of God, or letting God be God in us

For we are what he has made us, created in Christ Jesus.
EPHESIANS 2:10

You do not create God, God creates you.
St Irenaeus of Lyons[20]

Dorothy Parker is reputed to have quipped of someone, 'He was a self-made man and he worshipped his maker.' Christian community is not – and can never be – a human construct. It can never be achieved by human ideas or effort. *My* version of Christian community or *your* version or even *our* version can never be what God – who makes all things new – is seeking to create in us and through us. We need, in fact, to get out of the way of God. We need to be prepared to let go of 'our' plans to create 'our' vision of what 'our' church should be. The church is not ours but God's. Bonhoeffer, in his *Life Together*, warns:

> He who loves his dream of a community more than the Christian community itself becomes a destroyer of the latter, even though his personal intentions be ever so honest and earnest and sacrificial.[21]

Samuel Taylor Coleridge has a similar insight, albeit expressed a little differently, in his *Aids to Reflection* (1873):

> He who begins by loving Christianity better than Truth, will proceed by loving his own Sect or Church better than Christianity, and end by loving himself better than all.[22]

Coleridge's words carry conviction, I believe, if we take 'Christianity' here to mean *what humans have made of Christ rather than Christ himself*, who is in fact *the* truth. So, to let Christ be formed in us, we need to get out of the way of God. We need to let God be God. We need, in fact, Bonhoeffer argues, to be 'disillusioned' with all human ideas about community, including our own, before we are ready to hand our lives as living stones to God who will build his community, the church, in us and through us. It seems that God continues to build best *ex nihilo*, from nothing, from the dust, as we noted earlier. Søren Kierkegaard wrote, 'God creates everything out of nothing and everything which God is to use, he first reduces to nothing.'[23] Christian community grows from lives that are handed to God, from lives that are willing, in the words of John the Baptist, to decrease that God may increase in them.

There are times also when we need to get out of the way of God when we pray. Christian community grows through lives fertilised by the Holy Spirit through prayer. 'This mystery,' writes Paul, 'is Christ in you' (Colossians 1:27). All true prayer is the work of God in us, of Christ in us, of the Spirit within us. It is comforting to know that even when we don't know how to pray, the Spirit prays within us with groans too deep for words (Romans 8:26–27). There are times too when, in prayer, it is important to let go of our own 'prayer lists' and just give space for God to be and to pray within us. This kind of prayer is expressed simply and beautifully in *The Cloud of Unknowing*: 'His will is that you should look at him and let him have his way.'[24] In a similar vein, Mother Maribel of Wantage, of the Community of St Mary the Virgin, writes:

> If Christ lives in us then he prays in us and our chief concern should be to provide him a place in which he can pray. We know the joy of slipping into a silent church out of the din and roar of the traffic. What joy for him to push open our swing doors and find in us a place of silence where he can pray his prayer.[25]

This prayer of silence and stillness gives space for God's creative work within us.

There is, in my experience, a growing hunger across the different traditions and denominations of the Christian family for greater depth in prayer and for the contemplative dimension. Alongside this, I sense something of a hunger for 'community' and a *corporate* discipline or rule of life. We need not only God, but we need also one another to grow up in Christ and to serve his kingdom. Inspiring many, Archbishop Justin Welby has recognised the foundational place of prayer in the renewal of the church's life and mission, and not only individual prayer but also corporate prayer, encouraging the development of new forms of monastic community. Such communities, many of them intentionally ecumenical, with a rhythm of prayer which includes corporate silence and an emphasis on hospitality, are beginning to emerge.

In my own experience, being together with other Christians, across denominations, in prayerful silence with God often does more to build unity and community than meetings which are all 'words'. For the Holy Spirit, the Spirit of unity, to work in us and to grow the unity which is God's gift among us, we need, regularly, both in prayer and also in our interactions with others, to get out of the driving seat.

———— ◆ ————

Pause to ponder

Come to him, a living stone… Let yourselves be built into a spiritual house, to be a holy priesthood.
1 PETER 2:4–5

Be transformed by the renewing of your minds.
ROMANS 12:2

His will is that you should look at him and let him have his way.
The Cloud of Unknowing[26]

If we will but let our God and Father work his will with us, there can be no limit to his enlargement of our existence.
George MacDonald[27]

Pause for prayer

Mary said… 'Let it be with me according to your word.'
LUKE 1:38

Create in me a clean heart, O God, and put a new and right spirit within me.
PSALM 51:10

A new heart I will give you, and a new spirit I will put within you.
EZEKIEL 36:26

Jesus, Master Carpenter of Nazareth,
who on the cross through wood and nails
didst work our whole salvation:
Wield well thy tools in this thy workshop;
that we who come to thee rough hewn
may by thy hand be fashioned to a truer beauty and a greater
   usefulness.

———— ◆ ————

Communities of welcome

Welcome one another, therefore, just as Christ has welcomed
you, for the glory of God.
ROMANS 15:7

Occasionally, one still hears shaming stories of visitors to churches
who arrive and find a seat, only to be told, 'That's my seat; would you
mind moving?' The most attractive Christian communities – that is
to say, those which most attract people to Christ – are surely those
marked by humility, hospitality and an unconditional welcome.
Benedict, in his *Rule*, writes of 'a special welcome reserved for
those who are of the household of faith and for pilgrims'.[28] We are
to welcome others as those who have been welcomed by Christ, just
as we have been. Benedict goes further in exhorting the brothers to
welcome the guest as Christ himself.

Perhaps the reality and authenticity of our welcome of others in
Jesus' name depends to a degree on our knowing ourselves, not
only in our heads but also in our hearts, as welcomed by Christ. Paul
Tillich, the American theologian, encapsulates what he sees as the
heart of the gospel, and even the content of salvation, in exemplary
jargon-free language: 'You are accepted. You are accepted. Accepted
by that which is greater than you. Simply accept the fact that you are
accepted.'[29] If this happens, he contends, we experience grace. Tillich

is clear that God's acceptance of us is unconditional, just as our acceptance of others should be. How much damage do we do if the message we give implicitly or explicitly is 'We will accept you if you believe this or that' or 'We will accept you if you do this or stop doing that' or simply – and this can be more subtle – 'If you *become* like us'? Not to recognise that every visitor and stranger has something to give is to take ourselves out of the movement of divine love in God the holy Trinity, where love is always being given and always being received and the stranger is always being welcomed.

Made in the image of God, the giver of all good gifts, we are made to give

In 1977, I worked at the youth camp on the island of Iona. Through the inspiration of George Macleod, the youth camp welcomed young people from all over the world, including from behind the Iron Curtain, as well as from Glasgow. For part of the season, young men from what was then called Borstal (a young offenders' institution) came up to Iona. I remember going to welcome them off the ferry and seeing some hard and contemptuous expressions on their faces and quite a bit of macho swaggering, as well as hearing a litany of swear words punctuating their vocabulary. What they did not know at the time was that each of them would be looking after another young person of the same age with a significant physical handicap. It was wonderful and moving to see how in the course of their time on the island these lads formed deep friendships with those they were helping, and to see, after about a week, how many of their faces had lost the hardness of expression with which they had arrived. These young men were changed on the inside because they had been *released to give*, to demonstrate that they had much to offer and that their support and friendship was highly valued. The farewells at the jetty at the end of this time were moving to behold and there was some shedding of tears. These young men were released inwardly and changed by their experience of giving. They received much in their giving.

In recent years, there has been much research into what makes for human well-being. Universities, British Columbia and Harvard among them, have conducted experiments on the difference in indices of well-being recorded between people who spend money on themselves and people who give money to those who need it. The results have consistently demonstrated that giving makes for well-being, including, as some research shows, physical well-being. I find myself smiling when 'secular' research reveals truths that confirm biblical or theological principles. Made in the image of God, who is love and the giver of all good gifts, we human beings are made also to love and to give. In so doing, we become more truly ourselves and those whom God, in his love, is calling us to be.

But how are we perceived as a church? Are we seen as those who think we have everything to give and nothing to receive, with everything to teach and nothing to learn? Or, more hopefully, are we perceived as those who reflect Christ's unconditional love for others and who have the humility to ask and receive from them? Jesus in his extraordinary humility asks the Samaritan woman for a drink. In so doing, he shows her – one who no doubt was rejected by so many for her faith and lifestyle, not to mention her gender, and one who can only get to the well at the hottest time of day that nobody else would choose – that she *matters* and has something to give, something to offer him.

'All tribes and peoples and languages'

Praise the Lord, all you nations! Extol him, all you peoples!
PSALM 117:1

Christ – for Christ plays in ten thousand places, lovely in limbs, and lovely in eyes not his, to the Father through the features of men's faces.
Gerard Manley Hopkins[30]

As God is both the God of Israel and of all races and nations, his oneness implies and expresses diversity. In creating a diversity of creatures, God looks and sees that this rich diversity is good. My own life and ministry have been enormously enriched by the huge cultural and ecumenical diversity I experienced during my training at the Bossey Ecumenical Institute. Here, there were 60 languages (if you include the tribal with the national) spoken among the community. At any given moment, we were somewhere between Babel and Pentecost! I was later privileged to serve in significantly multicultural parishes where the congregations reflected much of that rich cultural and ethnic diversity. This was both a great gift and enrichment to all of us within the congregation and also an important sign to those around us of the inclusivity of God's love, where *everyone* has a place. Monocultural congregations in multicultural parishes can, unwittingly perhaps, express a perceived or actual tribalism that excludes those who are different and whose very difference would enrich the quality of the Christian community.

What was extraordinary about the fledgling Christian communities founded by Paul was their diversity. In no other context would you find, in one community, slave and free, rich and poor, Jew and Gentile, male and female. Paul, furthermore, recognised that there could not and should not be simply one identical and universal Christian culture. Monocultural Christianity does not reflect the rich diversity of God and his people. The Holy Spirit is given to unite us *in* – not *apart* from – our rich cultural diversity. The Holy Spirit is not the Spirit of homogeneity. The Holy Spirit heals division but does not eradicate difference. Like Michelangelo uncovering the latent beauty hidden within the stone as he sculpts, so the Holy Spirit releases us to become the unique selves that only each of us can be. To be 'one in Christ' (Galatians 3:28) is therefore not to be confused with being 'the same in Christ'. This is true both for each of us Christians and for each Christian congregation. We have a common identity and family likeness in Christ, but we reflect this in a rich diversity of expressions.

So Paul does not tell Jewish followers of Christ to disown or reject or abandon all their Jewish practices. Equally, he is clear that Gentile Christians should not adopt practices distinctive only to Judaism. Both within and between Christian communities, there will be different cultural expressions of the one Christian faith. Paul recognised that Abraham is 'father of all of us' (Romans 4:16), that is, of Jews and Gentiles, of people of every single race and culture on earth. The one God and Father of us all is worshipped in a huge variety of cultural expressions.

While recognising this, Paul had, nonetheless, to face the challenge of Christian tribalism. Among the Christ-followers in Corinth, it was already a clear and present danger. Some saw their primary allegiance as being to a particular person – Paul or Cephas or Apollos, for example – and not to Christ. We can see something of this throughout history and even today when 'parties' or 'schools' of Christians assert moral, theological or spiritual superiority over all others, claiming to be the one true church. This of course can happen not only between Christian denominations but also *within* them. Paul himself was subject to such judgementalism from the so-called 'super-spiritual' (*pneumatikoi*) in Corinth, who derided his claim to apostolic status, because, in their view, true apostles would never have to suffer the way that Paul had suffered. Paul exhorts them – and us, in our day – to make space for those who are different: 'Our heart is wide open to you… In return… open wide your hearts also' (2 Corinthians 6:11, 13). The Holy Spirit comes 'to open wide our hearts', to make us bigger, more spacious people – more spacious for God and more spacious for others.

———— ◆ ————

Pause to ponder

> In those days ten men from nations of every language shall take hold of a Jew, grasping his garment and saying, 'Let us go with you, for we have heard that God is with you.'
> ZECHARIAH 8:23

Are we becoming bigger, more compassionate people, expressing the wideness of God's mercy? Or, on the other hand, have we settled for safety and familiarity?

Are we being enriched by the great diversity of God's people, or have we become birds of a feather flocking together?

Pause for prayer

> After this I looked, and there was a great multitude that no one could count, from every nation, from all the tribes and peoples and languages, standing before the throne and before the Lamb.
> REVELATION 7:9

> For he is our peace… and has broken down the dividing wall, that is, the hostility between us.
> EPHESIANS 2:14

Father, who has made all people in your likeness
and love all whom you have made,
do not allow us to separate ourselves from you
by building barriers of race or colour.
As your Son, our Saviour, was born of a Hebrew mother,
but rejoiced in the faith of a Syrian woman
and of a Roman soldier,
welcomed the Greeks who looked for him
and allowed an African to carry his cross,
so teach us to see all people of every race and nation
as inheritors of the kingdom of your Son, Jesus Christ our Lord.

Toc H prayer

Jesus' question to us: 'If you greet only your brothers and sisters, what more are you doing than others?' (Matthew 5:47).

The Sending (Solomon Raj)

Go… And remember, I am with you always, to the end of the age.

MATTHEW 28:19–20

4

Turning outwards:
in love to God's world

The spaciousness of God

The Virgin of the Sign (Sister Lara Sacco)

Thy womb became more spacious than the heavens, containing the uncontainable.

Orthodox Hymn to Mary, Mother of God

God, the Holy Trinity, in creating, redeeming and leading is one who makes space *for* his people and *in* his people.

God, the creator

> He gives to all the creatures living on earth vast spaces, springs, rivers, forests.
> Gregory of Nazianzus[1]

In the account of creation in Genesis 1, creation takes place by separation: separation of light from darkness, separation of the waters above from the waters below, separation of the waters from the dry land. In these separations, God makes space for his creatures. In the space of the sky, God puts the two great lights and the lesser lights; in the space of the air, birds; in the space of the waters, fish; in the space of the land, animals; and finally, as the culmination of his creation, he creates humanity in his own image, giving them space to enjoy relationship with himself, with each other, with his creatures and indeed his creation. Olivier Clément writes: 'In the creative act itself, God in some manner limits himself, he withdraws to give human beings space in which to be free.'[2]

God, the redeemer

> He brought me out into a spacious place; he rescued me because he delighted in me.
> PSALM 18:19 (NIV)

> So if the Son makes you free, you will be free indeed.
> JOHN 8:36

> For freedom Christ has set us free.
> Galatians 5:1

The root of the Hebrew and Arabic word for salvation, variously rendered Jeshuah, Yasha and Jesus, actually means 'be capacious, make wide, make spacious'.[3] Jesus is the name of the one who delivers his people from slavery into freedom, from confinement into space. Miroslav Volf writes, 'On the cross God renews the covenant by making space for humanity in God's very self.'[4] Jesus, in his redeeming love, comes to makes space for us to live in him, in his capacious love, and to enjoy true freedom in him: 'Abide in me as I abide in you' (John 15:4). Paul's most common description of Christian identity is of those who live 'in Christ' and those in whom Christ lives, 'Christ in us'. In Christ, we are invited to discover 'the glorious liberty of the children of God' (Romans 8:21, KJV), inhabiting the space won for us by Christ's redeeming love. As Colin Gunton puts it:

> The calling of the community of reconciliation is to be those who learn to live in the space won for the life of the world by the victory of Jesus. Then and only then will it be able to open up space in which others may find freedom.[5]

As those given space by God, we are called to be space-*makers* for others.

God, the Holy Spirit

> You will know the truth, and the truth will make you free.
> JOHN 8:32

> Where the Spirit of the Lord is, there is freedom.
> 2 CORINTHIANS 3:17

> Just as what brings heat makes things expand, so it is the gift of love to stretch hearts wide open.
> St John Chrysostom[6]

In the Church of England ordination service, the bishop enjoins the ordinands to pray earnestly for the Holy Spirit 'that your heart may daily be enlarged and your understanding of the scriptures enlightened'. To see as God sees, we need the horizons of our hearts and minds to be enlarged. The Holy Spirit comes to make us bigger people in heart and mind, more capacious for God and for others. Paul urges the judgemental factions in Corinth not to be made smaller by judging others in the body of Christ, but to open wide their hearts as he has opened his hearts to them (2 Corinthians 6:11–13). Father Benson, founder of the Society of St John the Evangelist – the 'Cowley Fathers' – writes:

> The Holy Spirit accommodates himself to our littleness that we might respond to his greatness. We must know the pain of expansion… We are stretched indeed not on the rack of human torture but on the glorious being of the Holy Spirit.[7]

To be one with God is, through the Holy Spirit, to be liberated, not from our cultural milieu, because God works in and through culture, but from those personal and tribal prejudices that prevent us from discovering the depth and breadth of God's love. To be one with God, through prayer and stillness, through true repentance and praise and through love for one another is to be united *in God's love for the world*. God's love is outward bound, embracing the whole inhabited earth. To be one with God is to have the tribal blinkers removed from our eyes.

Fruitful witness in God's mission flows from worship 'in spirit and truth' (John 4:24). To withdraw to 'the desert place' to pray is not to escape the realities of the world; it is to discern them more clearly and to equip ourselves to engage with them more effectively in prayer and action. This time alone with God, Jesus emphasises, is an essential foundation of Christian life and witness. But this is not a call to a cloistered escapism. We do not go into solitude to be alone but to deepen our relationship with God in his love for and solidarity with the whole inhabited earth. The contemplative dimension of prayer, in opening us up to the love and presence of God, inspires and fertilises our witness in the world, which God so loves.

The space we give to God in prayer allows God to enlarge our hearts, enlighten our minds and make us more spacious for others. As with trees, the deeper our roots in God, the wider our branches can extend with his love. As those given space by God and in God, we are to make space for others; as those forgiven, to forgive; as those reconciled, to reconcile; as those given hospitality by God, to offer hospitality to others. Pope John Paul II captured this beautifully when he said, 'We need heralds of the gospel who are experts in humanity, who have shared to the full the joys and hopes, the anguish and the sadness of our day, but who are at the same time contemplatives in love with God.'[8] Our witness is to Christ, who has broken down the dividing wall (Ephesians 2:14).

From *xenophobia* to *philoxenia*: from fear of strangers to love of strangers

The Hospitality of Abraham and Sarah (Bose Monastery)

Do not neglect to show hospitality to strangers, for by doing that some have entertained angels without knowing it.
HEBREWS 13:2

Pray that none will be offended if I seek to make the Christian religion an inn where all are received joyously rather than a cottage where some few friends of the family are to be received.
Richard Hooker (1554–1600)[9]

The Trinity (Andrei Rublev)

When Jesus says that the one who will make his/her life secure will lose it (Luke 17:33), the word used for 'make secure' is from *peripoien*, meaning literally 'to make around'. The image is of putting boundary markers around us, thereby keeping our identity secure behind them. But security is a dangerous goal in the spiritual life, especially if it is the illusory security of 'knowing we are right' or the tribal security of 'birds of a feather flocking together' or the fearful security based on keeping the stranger out. The now world-famous Trinity icon by Rublev is called 'The icon of *Philoxenia*'. It communicates the hospitality of God, the Holy Trinity, who welcomes the stranger in. The visual 'language' of the icon draws on the hospitality of Abraham and Sarah, as described in Genesis 18, where, by the oaks of Mamre, they welcome in and provide for three strangers whom they later discover to be God. The hospitality of God invites us to be 'participants in the divine nature' (2 Peter 1:4), the life of the Holy Trinity, where love is always being given and always being received. Our hospitality to the stranger, echoing the hospitality of Sarah and Abraham, is at the same time hospitality to God whom we meet in the stranger. As strangers ourselves who have been welcomed by God, we welcome strangers, in God's name. In welcoming strangers, we welcome God.

The indiscriminate love of God

> For he makes his sun rise on the evil and on the good, and sends rain on the righteous and on the unrighteous.
> MATTHEW 5:45

This welcome – God's welcome, and our welcome of others in his name – is a welcome to *all*. There is no one outside or beyond its reach. God's love is indiscriminate. Gregory of Nyssa declared that in every human being, no matter what their background or beliefs, the faithful Christian discerns one for whom Christ died. I remember well making a pilgrimage to the Julian shrine in Norwich in 1986, where I had the privilege of spending time with Father Robert Llewellyn, the Guardian, who has done a great deal to make accessible the writings of Mother Julian. The day I saw him, he was overflowing with excitement at a particular scripture that had come to life for him in a new way. We are to love our enemies and pray for those who persecute us. We are to be and to act as children of our heavenly Father who 'makes his sun rise on the evil and on the good, and sends rain on the righteous and on the unrighteous' (Matthew 5:45). God's love is radically and shockingly inclusive. It does not favour the religious. As the apostle Peter painfully discovered, God has no favourites (Acts 10:34). God is no respecter of persons, religious or otherwise. (In parentheses, we might say that although in contemporary western church life, this word 'inclusive' has been appropriated by a particular and significant movement within the church, God's inclusivity obviously also embraces those who challenge these views. Wherever we stand and whatever our views, God's love includes our enemies. To avoid the dangers of tribalism, we must recognise this.)

When Emperor Julian, some 50 years after the conversion of Constantine, tried to eliminate Christian faith from the empire, he did not succeed. Lamenting his failure, he wrote, 'These impious Galileans [meaning Christians] look after not only their own but ours as well.'[10] They demonstrated that God's love is not sectarian or tribal. Looking after our own, though important, indeed essential, is not enough. Paul, in his letters, evidently laboured by every means to urge a unity and mutuality of love and service within and among the Christ-following communities he founded. He was, however, equally clear that God's love is to be demonstrated also to those *outside* these communities: 'Whenever we have an opportunity, let us work for the good of all' (Galatians 6:10). Christ followers are to show 'hospitality to strangers' (Romans 12:13), to be 'kindly to everyone' (2 Timothy 2:24), to let their 'gentleness be known to everyone' (Philippians 4:5) and 'to be gentle, and to show every courtesy to everyone' (Titus 3:2).

———— ◆ ————

Pause to ponder

Enlarge the site of your tent, and let the curtains of your habitations be stretched out; do not hold back; lengthen your cords and strengthen your stakes.

ISAIAH 54:2

Then people will come from east and west, from north and south, and will eat in the kingdom of God.

LUKE 13:29

Remember, the Lord invites us all; and since he is truth Itself, we cannot doubt him.

St Teresa of Ávila[11]

There's a wideness in God's mercy,
like the wideness of the sea;
there's a kindness in God's justice,
which is more than liberty.

Frederick Faber (1814–63)

Pause for prayer

You shall love the alien as yourself, for you were aliens in the land of Egypt: I am the Lord your God.

LEVITICUS 19:34

Behind the Barbed Wire (Solomon Raj)

O God, break open my heart so that the whole world may fall in.

Mother Teresa of Calcutta

———— ◆ ————

Brothers and sisters in humanity

We must pray not that others be converted to us but that we all may be drawn closer to Christ. The spiritual horizon for prayer for unity is not merely Christianity, it is the redemption of humankind.

Father Paul Couturier[12]

Any man's death diminishes me because I am involved in
mankind.
John Donne[13]

There is a plurality of those who share in the same human
nature… but in all of them, humanity is one.
St Gregory of Nyssa[14]

In the face of the diabolical violence perpetrated by terrorist groups
in the past months and years, it has surely been in God's will and
purposes that Christian leaders have spoken out not only for
Christian victims but also for Yazidi and Muslim ones, the latter being
easily the greatest in number in the Middle East. Our solidarity as
Christians with persecuted Christians – to which we as Christians in
the west have so often failed to witness – is not a tribal solidarity
which excludes others. It is rather a necessary sign and a foretaste of
the unity to which Christ calls all, that is to say every human being of
every race and culture, a unity in which, ultimately, Christ 'is all and
in all' (Colossians 3:11).

A monk is someone who is separated from everything and united to everybody[15]

The desert fathers and mothers knew that, in their call to a life
of prayer in the desert, they were not escaping the world, but
entering more deeply into God's love for the world and engaging
in the spiritual struggle through prayer for the whole world. In this
prayer in the desert, through apprehending more fully God's love
and longing for the salvation of the world, when Christ shall be 'all
in all', they discovered and entered into a deep prayerful solidarity
with all humanity. So Anthony of Egypt could write, 'Our salvation is
with our neighbour. We are all of one substance and members one
of another, for he who loves his neighbour loves God and he who
loves God loves his own soul.'[16] Centuries later, William Tyndale
wrote, 'To thy neighbour, thou owest thine heart, thyself and all that

thou hast and can do.'[17] Matthew Arnold quotes Thomas Wilson, the 18th-century Bishop of Sodor and Man, 'It is not so much in our neighbour's interest that we love him but ours. Our salvation does in some measure depend on that of others.'[18] The 20th-century Russian saint, Silouan the Athonite, writes, 'Blessed is the soul who loves her brother/sister, for her brother/sister is her life.'[19] Then, echoing the apostle Paul's words on solidarity, 'When one member suffers, all suffer', he writes, 'The suffering of the other is my suffering, my neighbour's healing is my healing, my brother's glory will be my glory.'[20]

We see this love of Christ that has broken down the dividing walls in the life and witness of Edith Cavell, an Anglican nurse from Norfolk. Cavell served in German-occupied Belgium in World War I. She nursed all who were wounded, saving the lives not only of Allied troops but also those of the Germans without discrimination. She was accused by the Germans of treason for saving the lives of some wounded Allied troops by helping them escape to Holland. When facing execution by firing squad, she said:

> I have no fear of shrinking. I have seen death so often that it is not strange or fearful to me. This I would say, standing as I do in view of God and eternity… I realise that patriotism is not enough. I must have no hatred or bitterness towards anyone.[21]

We see such solidarity across divisions of nationality, inspired by Christian faith, also in Mother Maria Skobtsova. When the Jews were being targeted by the Nazis in Paris and forced to wear the Star of David, Mother Maria wrote, 'If we were true Christians we would all wear the Star.'[22] In March 1945, she herself was taken to Ravensbrück and it is said that she voluntarily took the place of another woman going into the gas chamber. Mother Maria was martyred not for her solidarity with Christians but with Jews, her costly witness expressing God's deep love for all humanity.

———— ◆ ————

Pause to ponder

From one ancestor he made all nations to inhabit the whole earth.
ACTS 17:26

And I, when I am lifted up from the earth, will draw all people to myself.
JOHN 12:32

We must be saved together. We must come to God together. Together we must all return to the Father's house. What would God say to us if some of us came to him without the others?
Charles Péguy[23]

Pause for prayer

Lord Jesus Christ,
help us to see in each one we meet
a sister or brother in your image,
one for whom you lived and died and rose again,
a child of your own redeeming,
precious in your sight and called by name.

The Sending (Solomon Raj)

Crossing boundaries: 'Lambs into the midst of wolves'

Go on your way. See, I am sending you out like lambs into the midst of wolves.

LUKE 10:3

Walk in wisdom toward those who are outside, redeeming the time.

COLOSSIANS 4:5 (NKJV)

> I cannot praise a fugitive and cloistered virtue, unexercised and unbreathed, that never sallies out and sees her adversary, but slinks out of the race where that immortal garland is to be run for, not without dust and heat.
>
> John Milton[24]

I discovered recently that a mother eagle, if the eaglets are reluctant to leave the nest and to fly, goes out to find sharp or uncomfortable things and puts them in the nest. To become eagles, eaglets need to get out of the comfort of the nest and learn to fly. On a similar avian theme, I saw in a shop window in Kenilworth, in a suitably heated and ventilated glass container, some baby chicks. There was a sign on the window, which read, 'If they are not moving, it means that they are asleep.' This sign, I thought, could suitably adorn every church porch!

As a called people, we are also a *sent* people. Jesus says, 'Come', and Jesus says, 'Go'. God, who in Christ has crossed all boundaries and broken down the dividing walls (Ephesians 2:14), calls us too to cross boundaries. We are called to leave behind our comfortable familial, tribal, even ecclesial securities to go where we will be vulnerable, as 'lambs in the midst of wolves'. This feels like dangerous territory, where we can no longer rely on our own supposed strengths or the false security of being 'in charge' or even in 'control'. It is where we have to trust in God and God alone. This is, by definition, *precarious* living. This word is especially apt, having its root in the Latin *preces* or 'prayers'. Participating in the life and mission of God is all about our vulnerable, prayerful – and confident – dependence on God. Simon Tugwell describes the life of Francis of Assisi as one of 'radical unprotectedness'.[25] The church is truly the church when it is not securely church-centric, depending on the respectability or influence of the church, but rather when it is precariously Christocentric, living and witnessing in daily dependence on the Holy Spirit, in the world for which Christ died. It should not surprise us that the church usually grows most when it is unprotected by any worldly status or power or when it is under persecution.

Teenagers often used to say to their parents, 'You need to get out more!': words, perhaps, for many of us in the church, who seek comfort more than transformation. We need to get out more, out of our comfort zones. When the 70 return, having been sent out 'like lambs in the midst of wolves', they are overflowing with joy (Luke 10:17). They have experienced the extraordinary provision of God, which was given them when – *and not before* – they dared to trust and obey the command of Jesus. It is in this dangerous, unprotected living, out of our comfort zones, that this discovery happens. But how many of us actually dare to cross boundaries? From being lambs in the midst of sheep to lambs in the midst of wolves? How many of us dare to get out of our trenches and go into 'no-man's land', let alone into 'enemy' territory, where we have to rely utterly upon God? How many of us dare to leave behind our personal, social or theological securities to become 'radically unprotected', 'like lambs in the midst of wolves'?

Martin Luther writes words which disturb the insidious comfort we are tempted to inhabit:

> The kingdom of God is to be in the midst of your enemies. And those who will not suffer this do not want to be of the kingdom of Christ; they want to be among friends, to sit among roses and lilies not with the bad people but with the devout people. O you blasphemers and betrayers of Christ! If Christ had done what you are doing, who would ever have been spared?[26]

Reconciliation

The ministry of reconciliation is all about crossing boundaries. The word Paul uses for reconciliation is *katallagein* (noun) or *katalasso* (verb). The root of these words is *allos*, meaning 'other'. *Alasso* means 'to make otherwise', 'to alter'. It indicates change or even exchange. *Kata* can mean not only 'down', the opposite of *ana*, meaning 'up', but it can also mean 'alongside'. So, one interpretation of Paul's understanding of reconciliation might be 'to get alongside the one who is other'. As Christians, we are called to be, in the language of Barth, reconciled reconcilers. This is a closely scriptural interpretation of the heart of our call as Christians. When Paul writes, in 2 Corinthians 5:19, that 'in Christ God was reconciling the world to himself, not counting their trespasses against them, and *entrusting the message of reconciliation to us*', the literal translation of this last phrase is 'having placed *within us*' the message of reconciliation. Paul is speaking not simply of the *idea* of reconciliation but of the *experience* of reconciliation. Paul is saying that those who have themselves received and experienced the reconciliation accomplished by Christ are called to be ambassadors for Christ. For Paul, reconciliation is not a *human* gift to be given. It is not and can never be a human accomplishment. Reconciliation is a gift of God, accomplished by Christ. Those who have received and appropriated this gift are called to share it. They/we are called, as reconciled reconcilers, to cross boundaries, to go to 'the other', to make space for the other. This means taking risks and crossing boundaries for the gospel's sake.

Love of enemies

> I say to you that listen, Love your enemies, do good to those who hate you.
> LUKE 6:27

St Silouan of Athos describes love of our enemies as the one 'criterion of true faith'.[27] This above all, Silouan writes, expresses our likeness to Christ who, on the cross, prayed, 'Father, forgive them, for they know not what they do.' Silouan goes further, too, saying that if we do not pray for our enemies, we lose the grace of God. Jesus calls us to love our enemies and to bless those who persecute us. But how is this possible? How was it possible for Stephen, being stoned to death, to pray, 'Lord, do not hold this sin against them' (Acts 7:60)? The short answer, as bitter experience may have told us, is that it is not possible. At least, without God's help, without the Holy Spirit, it is not possible. 'The one who does not possess the Holy Spirit,' Silouan writes, 'has no desire to pray for his or her enemies.'[28] It is only God's love at work in us that can give us the desire and capacity to pray for our enemies.

Most of us will know all too well how far we fall short here. If we are honest, we may want to recognise that we do not even want to pray for, let alone to love, our enemies. But to face this, to acknowledge our failure to love and to bless our enemies and then to seek God's grace to do so, brings us back to a place of hope. We can be encouraged and inspired by the grace of God at work in the lives and witness of others. The Serbian bishop, Nikolaj Velimirović, who met with Silouan at St Panteleimon Monastery on Mount Athos, was given grace to see how his enemies, who were many, could draw him to a deeper dependence on God. In his beautiful 'Prayers by the Lake', he writes:

> Bless my enemies, O Lord, and I bless them and do not curse them. My enemies have driven me more into your arms than my friends have. My friends have bound me to the earth; my enemies have loosened my bonds from the earth and have destroyed all my hopes in the world. Bless my enemies, Lord, and I bless them.[29]

In the BBC Christmas broadcast of 1940, less than six weeks after the bombing of Coventry and the destruction of the cathedral, Provost Richard Howard said:

> What we want to tell the world is this: that with Christ born again in our hearts today, we are trying, hard as it may be, to banish all thoughts of revenge… We are going to try to make a kinder, a simpler, a more Christ-child-like sort of world in the days beyond this strife.[30]

One of the most inspiring recent examples of this love of enemies comes from the martyrdom of the seven Trappist brothers in Tibhirine, Algeria in 1996. Their story is told with extraordinary conviction and power in the film *Of Gods and Men*. These seven brothers, having been threatened by armed men and knowing of the threat to their lives, chose to stay in their monastery, living a life of simplicity, poverty and prayer, serving the needs of the very poor Muslims living around them. Knowing the probability of their imminent death, Father Christian de Chergé wrote in his Spiritual Testament: 'I hope when the time comes to be conscious enough to ask pardon from God and from my brothers in humanity, and at the same time to forgive my aggressor with all my heart.' In words addressed to the unknown one who is to kill him – he knew that he would be killed – he writes:

> And for you too, friend of the last hour, who did not know what you were doing, I wish this Thank You and A-DIEU and that we may meet again as happy thieves in Paradise, if it pleases God, the Father of us all. Amen.[31]

Pause to ponder

> Bless those who persecute you; bless and do not curse them.
> ROMANS 12:14

> I am the enemy you killed, my friend.
> Wilfred Owen[32]

> *They drew a circle that shut me out –*
> *Heretic, rebel, a thing to flout.*
> *But Love and I had the wit to win:*
> *We drew a circle that took them in.*
> Charles Edwin Markham[33]

There will never be beings unloved by God, since God is absolute love.

Hans Urs von Balthasar[34]

Pause for prayer

All have sinned and fall short of the glory of God.

ROMANS 3:23

The Coventry Litany of Reconciliation

The hatred which divides nation from nation, race from race, class from class,
Father, forgive.

The covetous desires of people and nations to possess what is not their own,
Father, forgive.

The greed which exploits the work of human hands and lays waste the earth,
Father, forgive.

Our envy of the welfare and happiness of others,
Father, forgive.

Our indifference to the plight of the imprisoned, the homeless, the refugee,
Father, forgive.

The lust which dishonours the bodies of men, women and children,
Father, forgive.

The pride which leads us to trust in ourselves and not in God,
Father, forgive.

Be kind to one another, tender-hearted, forgiving one another,
as God in Christ has forgiven you.

EPHESIANS 4:32

Jesus' question to us: 'If you love those who love you, what reward
do you have?' (Matthew 5:46).

Evangelism and Mercy (Solomon Raj)

May I never boast of anything except the cross of our Lord Jesus Christ, by which the world has been crucified to me, and I to the world.

GALATIANS 6:14

5

Turning to the cross

Cruciformity

I want to know Christ and the power of his resurrection and the sharing of his sufferings by becoming like him in his death.
PHILIPPIANS 3:10

Whoever does not carry the cross and follow me cannot be my disciple.
LUKE 14:27

It is to the cross that the Christian is challenged to follow his/ her Master. No path of redemption can make a path around it.
Hans Urs von Balthasar[1]

The poet Rainer Maria Rilke writes, in 'The Swan', of a 'letting go of the land that we stand on and cling to every day'.[2] There is an inescapable cruciformity to all Christian life. Jesus calls us to take up our cross *daily* and to follow him (Luke 9:23). When I visited St Paul's monastery on Mount Athos many years ago, I read outside the monastery the words: 'Unless you die before you die, you will die when you die.' At the very heart of the call of Jesus is the call to die, to lose one's life to find it. Dietrich Bonhoeffer wrote, 'When Christ calls someone, he bids him/her come and die.'[3] This is the way of the cross, the way into resurrection life.

The apostle Paul

> I have been crucified with Christ; and it is no longer I who live,
> but it is Christ who lives in me.
> GALATIANS 2:19–20

> Dying, and yet we live.
> 2 CORINTHIANS 6:9 (NIV)

Paul knew and experienced at a deep level that death and resurrection are inseparable. 'For while we live, we are always being given up to death for Jesus' sake, so that the life of Jesus may be made visible in our mortal flesh' (2 Corinthians 4:11). Later in the same letter, Paul expresses it simply and directly, 'Dying, and yet we live' (2 Corinthians 6:9, NIV). The great preacher John Henry Jowett (1863–1923), in one of his sermons, told of how he had been out walking in snow-covered mountains and had seen the bloodstained track of a wounded hare. He reflected that that bloodstained track and that wounded hare were Paul on his journeys across Europe. Certainly, Paul knew – and this theme is woven deep within 2 Corinthians – the paradox of God's grace and power being released in and through human frailty, struggle and affliction.

> We have this treasure in clay jars… We are afflicted in every
> way, but not crushed.
> 2 CORINTHIANS 4:7–8

> We are treated as imposters, and yet are true; as unknown,
> and yet are well known; as dying, and see – we are alive… as
> sorrowful, yet always rejoicing; as poor, yet making many rich;
> as having nothing, and yet possessing everything.
> 2 CORINTHIANS 6:8–10

It is as if Paul is saying we need to be humbled, afflicted, broken of any egotism, and stripped of our vanity and wilfulness before we can experience God's power in us or through us. We have to be clear and with no room for doubt 'that this extraordinary power belongs to God and does not come from us' (2 Corinthians 4:7). Archbishop Michael Ramsey, in an address given to those about to be ordained as priests, is perhaps highlighting something of this same dynamic when he says:

> Here is a priest, so cheerful, always cheerful, cheerful for the wrong reasons, cheerful in pride and shallowness; he may be liked and admired, *but he will not become a true priest until his heart is broken*, whether in penitence before his Lord or in agony for the people he is serving.[4]

Jesus said, 'Woe to you when all speak well of you' (Luke 6:26).

So we see that resurrection life does not follow crucifixion as if in a separate category chronologically or spiritually. They are inseparable. Archbishop Anastasios of Albania, who has witnessed extraordinary resurrection life emerge through the martyrdom of many faithful Christians and the destruction of so many churches and monasteries in Albania under the severest communist persecution, affirms that as Christians 'we are called to an existential participation in the death and life of Christ'.[5] In his final command and commission, Jesus says, 'You will receive power when the Holy Spirit has come upon you; and you will be my witnesses in Jerusalem, in all Judea and Samaria, and to the ends of the earth' (Acts 1:8). Witness, as the New Testament Greek word for it, *martyr*, suggests, is intrinsically costly. God promises his people in exile, through the prophecies of Isaiah, 'When you pass through the waters, I will be with you; and through the rivers, they shall not overwhelm you; when you walk through fire you shall not be burned, and the flame shall not consume you' (Isaiah 43:2). The promise is not '*if* you' but '*when* you'.

That trials lie ahead is a given. It is inevitable. Jesus warns the disciples, 'In the world you face persecution. But take courage; I have conquered the world' (John 16:33). The New Testament Greek can equally translate as, 'In the world you have affliction', the point being that faithful witness is costly whether or not it leads to persecution, a particular form of affliction. Trouble, affliction or persecution is promised but so also is the presence and grace of God in the midst of such things. Mother Julian encapsulates this so well: 'He did not say, "You will not be tempest-tossed, you will not be wearied, you will not be distressed." He said, "You will not be overcome."'[6]

So there can be no space for 'prosperity' gospels that promise riches – not least the financial kind – but bypass the call of Jesus to take up the cross daily. It means that there can be no place for any 'Christian' message that attributes all human suffering to the sin of the sufferer(s) or any lack of physical healing after prayer to lack of faith. Paul knew that his limitations and afflictions, far from being an obstacle to his apostolic calling and missionary fruitfulness, were, in the economy of God, central to the grace and power of God working through him (2 Corinthians 12:9). Like Jacob before him, who, having wrestled with God, was left limping, Paul had agonised and wrestled with the principalities and powers and what God's purposes could be in his struggles and humiliations. Again and again, he had prayed urgently that 'the thorn in his flesh' – whatever this was – would be taken away. This did not happen. Paul had to learn the sufficiency of God's grace not *apart* from his trials but *within* them.

'The crucified mind, not the crusading mind'

In the same way, there can be no place for 'crusading' or imperialistic theology or missionary engagement where the impulse is dominance rather than love, or where others are not seen or treated as brothers or sisters for whom Christ died. Kosuke Koyama, in the face of the devastation of Hiroshima and Nagasaki struck by atomic bombs, writes, 'biblical truth is not an "intact" truth, but a *suffered* truth'.[7] He goes on, 'The crucified mind, not the crusading mind, must it not be the mind of missionaries, indeed of all Christians.'

For Paul, to be daily transformed by the renewal of our minds, to acquire the mind of Christ, we are to 'take every thought captive to obey Christ' (2 Corinthians 10:5). There needs to be a continual self-emptying and turning back to Christ (Philippians 2). Without this *metanoia*, this change of mind, our thinking and our witness will likely revert to the level of natural human thinking, what Paul describes as *kata sarka*, and not be according to the Spirit, *kata pneuma*. Put more simply, there is a need for a daily surrender of our wills to God, a revolution from 'God on my terms' to 'me on God's terms'. This is the same revolution we are invited to make whenever we pray, 'Thy kingdom come, thy will be done.'

For the theologian, the church leader or indeed any Christian, it is not actually about winning arguments or proving the other wrong. It is certainly not about capturing more territory for our cause by using the weapons of this world. We do not 'win' or advance the kingdom by force of arms, force of personality, force of intellect or even force of numbers or majority votes. In fact, we do not win by force at all. Why? Because, as Rilke writes, 'If we do win, it is a small victory, and the victory itself makes us small.'[8] We need rather to be brought to the place where we recognise the emptiness of all human victories, where we can hold lightly to the urge constantly to justify ourselves. There is nothing less attractive, and nothing less missionally attracting, surely, than Christians bashing each other – or anyone else for that matter – over the head with their own version of the truth. In such cases, C.S. Lewis' demon Screwtape would surely have responded with great enthusiasm, '*Quod erat demonstrandum*' – QED, point proved. As Isaac the Syrian puts it, 'If you've tasted the truth, you are not contentious for the truth.'[9]

The Holy Spirit, who leads us into the truth, works to release us from any egotistical need to be right at the expense of another or to be *proved* right. Jean Vanier quotes Patriarch Athenagoras of Constantinople (Ecumenical Patriarch, 1948–1972), who, experiencing the disarming love of God, writes, 'I am disarmed of the need to be right and to justify myself by disqualifying others.'[10]

To be disarmed of the compulsion to justify ourselves to others, to ourselves or to God would surely render our witness more attractive and attracting. The desert father John the Dwarf writes, 'We have put aside the easy burden which is self-accusation, and weighed ourselves down with the heavy one, self-justification'.[11] Have we personally, or corporately as the church, succumbed to the temptation of self-justification?

———— ◆ ————

Pause to ponder

All of us who have been baptised into Christ Jesus were baptised into his death.
ROMANS 6:3

The cross is not the terrible end to an otherwise god-fearing and happy life, but it meets us at the beginning of our communion with Christ.
Dietrich Bonhoeffer[12]

Life is the destiny you are bound to refuse until you have consented to die.
W.H. Auden[13]

Pause for prayer

Out of the depths I cry to you, O Lord. Lord, hear my voice!
PSALM 130:1–2

O Lord, make haste to help me!
PSALM 70:1

We adore you, O Christ, and we bless you.
Because by your holy cross you have redeemed the world.
From the Stations of the Cross

O Tree of Calvary,
send thy roots deep down into my heart.
Gather together the soil of my heart,
the sands of my fickleness,
the stones of my stubbornness,
the mud of my desires.
Bind them all together,
O Tree of Calvary,
interlace them with thy strong roots,
entwine them with the network of thy love.

Chandran Devanesen[14]

Holy God, holy and strong, holy and immortal, have mercy on us.

The Trisagion

———— ◆ ————

The inscrutability of God

Truly, you are a God who hides himself.

ISAIAH 45:15

Rouse yourself! Why do you sleep, O Lord?… Why do you hide your face?

PSALM 44:23–24

O Lord, why do you cast me off? Why do you hide your face from me?

PSALM 88:14

You have wrapped yourself with a cloud so that no prayer can pass through.

LAMENTATIONS 3:44

Sooner or later, life confronts us with the inscrutability of God. Having been drawn to Christ and responded in faith, the same God who draws us to himself withdraws, or rather withdraws from our sight, our sense and our awareness. We think we can 'read' the ways of God and then discover that we cannot. Having discovered and experienced that God can and does protect and provide, we later experience what feels like the absence of his protection and provision. Having experienced that God can and does answer prayer, sometimes in the most wonderful and extraordinary ways, we discover that our prayers are not always answered in the ways or timing we expected or even longed for, or apparently not answered at all. So we can feel – and actually be – more vulnerable *after* we have begun our Christian journey than before. Our securities have been stripped away. We do not see that this stripping down may actually be within God's purposes, drawing us into a deeper and more courageous dependence and, therefore, in a way that is hidden from us at the time, a gift and an opportunity. We discover, in short, that the God who reveals himself is at the same time the God who conceals himself.

C.S. Lewis writes in the first of his 'Narnia Chronicles', *The Magician's Nephew*, of a boy called Digory, whose mother is dying. When he first encounters the great lion Aslan, he pleads, 'Please will you give me some magic fruit of this country to make Mother well?' It is a prayer of real longing and urgency, which Aslan seems to ignore completely. Lewis writes, 'He had been desperately hoping that the Lion would say "Yes"; he had been horribly afraid it might say "No". But he was taken aback when it did neither.'[15] Lewis, as a boy aged ten, had watched his own mother dying of cancer. In the story, Digory pleads again for Aslan to cure his dying mother. Lewis writes:

> Up till then he had been looking at the Lion's great feet and the huge claws on them; now, in his despair, he looked up at its face. What he saw surprised him as much as anything in his whole life. For the tawny face was bent down near his own and great shining tears stood in the Lion's eyes. They were such big,

bright tears compared with Digory's own that for a moment he felt as if the Lion must really be sorrier about his Mother than he was himself.[16]

We might think of the tears of Jesus, so moved by the grief of Mary and Martha at the death of their brother and his own dear friend Lazarus.

We see, we know from our own experience – and the psalms make patently clear – that those who seek to trust God are not protected from grief, pain, darkness or dereliction. We are not sheltered from 'the darkest valley'; we are, however, assured of the presence of God with us in the midst of such experiences (Psalm 23:4). No matter where we are, no matter what life feels like, we cannot escape the presence of God: 'Where can I flee from your presence?' (Psalm 139:7); 'The darkness is not dark to you; the night is as bright as the day' (Psalm 139:12). While we seek the security of the light, where we can see what is going on in our lives and make some kind of sense of it, God calls us to trust him in the darkness. As Newman confesses:

I loved to choose and see my path,
but now lead Thou me on!
I loved the garish day, and spite of fears,
Pride ruled my will. Remember not past years.
John Henry Newman[17]

The words of Minnie Haskins, quoted by King George VI in his Christmas day broadcast in 1939, reflect the same theme:

I said to the man who stood at the Gate of the Year, 'Give me a light that I might tread safely into the unknown.' And he replied, '*Go out into the darkness and put your hand into the hand of God*. That shall be to you better than light and safer than a known way.'[18]

God, who is light, allows us to experience darkness, just as he, in Christ, has done. The good news of the gospel, the Easter faith we proclaim, is good news precisely because it is not escapism; it embraces and transfigures all that is, including the darkness. In the Christian faith, there can be no place for shallow optimism or the denial of darkness or death.

The Orthodox icon of the resurrection is also called 'Christ's Descent into Hell'.

The Orthodox Church proclaims, 'Christ is risen from the dead, trampling down death by death and upon those in the tomb bestowing life.' At Easter, the church sings to Christ crucified, who descended into hell and rose again, 'You have descended into the abyss of the earth, O Christ, and have broken down the eternal doors which imprison those who are bound, and like Jonah after three days in the whale, you have risen from the tomb.' In his descent into hell, Christ enters the deepest darkness that any of us could experience. He comes to draw us, beginning with Adam and Eve, out of darkness into his marvellous light. The icon assures us that there is no human condition or predicament outside or beyond his redeeming love.

In the extraordinary and luminous mosaics of Father Marko Rupnik,[19] he depicts in iconographic language the same event with Christ, who has harrowed hell, drawing Adam and Eve out of darkness into his resurrection light. Here, however, in Rupnik's depiction, Christ is drawing the hand of Eve into a wound in his own body. It speaks of the recreation of our fallen human nature in the wounds of Christ: 'By his wounds you have been healed' (1 Peter 2:24).

Detail from the Parvis of Ta' Pinu National Shrine (Centro Aletti)

The oyster

In the life of the oyster, it is the unwanted and uncomfortable grit that penetrates the oyster and causes it to weep 'tears' around it that leads to the formation of the pearl. Without this grit and the consequent 'tears' that flow, there is no pearl.

When I left school, I went to work at a Cheshire Home for people who were physically disabled. One evening, one of the volunteers had the bright idea of having a wheelchair race to the pub. The other volunteers, including myself, and those in wheelchairs, in the spirit of youthful levity and fun, agreed. I was pushing Brian, a delightful young man in his early 20s with muscular dystrophy. He was to become a great friend and more. At the time we left for the pub, it was getting dark. The race began. What I had not seen or anticipated was a pothole in the road. As I crossed the unexpected pothole at speed, the wheelchair tipped over. To my horror, Brian's face hit the tarmac. I was truly mortified. In response to my stupidity and negligence, Brian was so gracious and forgiving. Through the trauma of this event, of my guilt and his forgiveness, a depth of friendship grew. Some time later, after I had left, Brian contacted me. He was fearful of death, which he now knew to be imminent. We met. Though he would not then have described himself as a Christian, he asked me to pray. I felt totally inadequate but I did pray quietly and with real urgency for God to take away his fear. After a few minutes, as I was continuing in quiet prayer, Brian said, 'Thank you, I feel such peace now,' and looking at his face I could see it was true. That was a turning point. When it came to his death, he had both faith and peace. This eventuality, I am convinced, would not have happened were it not for the event that we would never have wished to happen: the turning over of the wheelchair on the road. So often we discover, in retrospect, the weaving of God's good purposes through events in our lives that we would never have chosen to happen and that have caused us or others considerable pain. Sometimes crises are extraordinary bearers of grace.

———— ◆ ————

Pause to ponder

We have this treasure in clay jars, so that it may be made clear that this extraordinary power belongs to God and does not come from us.

2 CORINTHIANS 4:7

Christ transfigures everything in us, the good as well as the bad. In every person there is a wound. Moan about it and it becomes a source of torment. Transfigured by Christ it becomes a source of energy and healing.

Brother Roger of Taizé[20]

Pause for prayer

O joy that seekest me through pain,
I cannot close my heart to thee;
I trace the rainbow through the rain,
and feel the promise is not vain,
that morn shall tearless be.
George Matheson[21]

———— ◆ ————

Being real with God

I've always been amused by the great preacher Charles Spurgeon's advice to preachers in training: 'When you speak of heaven, let your face light up. When you speak of hell, your ordinary face will do.'[22] I know, of course, what he is getting at, but there is a danger in the spiritual life of us 'putting on faces' to God or to others, or indeed to ourselves. To be alive and oxygenated by the Spirit, we need both to be real with God and also to let God be real with us.

Teresa of Ávila wrote, 'All difficulties in prayer can be traced to one cause, praying as if God were absent.'[23] Do we pray as if God were absent or present? Real or not real? I sometimes think of Matthew's gospel as a piece of Brighton rock with the same words written throughout, from the beginning to the middle and to the end: God is always with us. In the first chapter, we read the prophecy of Isaiah, '"Look, the virgin shall conceive and bear a son, and they shall name him Emmanuel", which means, "*God is with us*"' (Matthew 1:23). If we break open the gospel in the middle, we hear Jesus say, 'Where two or three are gathered in my name, *I am there among them*' (Matthew 18:20). Finally, at the end of the gospel are the very last words of the risen Jesus, 'And remember, *I am with you always*, to the end of the age' (Matthew 28:20). This is the reality, expressed so beautifully and profoundly in Psalm 139, of the inescapable presence of God.

Wherever we are, whatever the circumstances, we can celebrate with confidence that 'the Lord is here. His Spirit is with us.'

How real are we with God? Teresa of Ávila is also reputed to have said to God during a particularly difficult time, 'If this is how you treat your friends, no wonder you have so few of them!' How real are we with God? Do we speak to God by communicating what is really in us? Or are we too polite or 'religious'? As a parent, how would we feel if our child whom we loved beyond words only ever related to us by asking things from us? How would we feel if our child only spoke to us in formal language? How would we feel if our child never responded to our deep and unconditional love for them? We would surely long for our child to know our love, to be free and spontaneous with us, to laugh and to cry with us, to share with us their longings and their fears and sometimes to throw their arms around us in love.

Truly to worship God, or to worship God 'in Spirit and in truth', we need to recognise that God knows us better than we know ourselves. There is nothing about us, and nothing within us that is hidden from God. I sometimes think of the opening prayer in much Anglican Eucharistic worship, known as the Collect for Purity, as like the airport scanning doorways which detect anything on you or even inside you. We begin with the recognition that God, 'unto whom all hearts are open, all desires known and from whom no secrets are hidden', sees us, knows us and loves us so much more fully and truly than we could ever do. We can be and must be who we truly are with God. We don't have to change for God to love us. God loves and can only love the person we actually are. To believe that we need to be different for God to love us can be a subtle kind of pride. So it is helpful and good in prayer just to be who we really are with God. Contemplative prayer is all about this and letting God, who is infinitely bigger than any of our understandings, be with us in his love. If we do this, we may discover that God's love is a gently *transforming* love.

Letting God be real with us

Letting God be real with us means, of course, giving God space to be God in our lives. It means allowing God to speak to us, to feed us, to love us and to guide us. Relationships come unstuck when we do not invest in them. This means work. Orthodox theology is both ascetical and mystical. An image sometimes used is of a boat. As human beings, we need to row the boat out to where it is in a position to receive the wind of the Spirit in its sails. God invites us to cooperate as fellow workers, or, in the language of the New Testament, *synergountes*. For this synergy with God, there needs to be spiritual discipline. This necessarily involves the dimension of obedience. Benedict was acutely aware, when he wrote *The Rule*, of the danger of a freelance 'what suits me' monasticism. Referring to Sarabaite monks, he writes:

> For a rule of life they have only the satisfaction of their own desires. Any precept they think up for themselves and then decide to adopt they do not hesitate to call holy. Anything they dislike they consider inadmissible.[24]

There is perhaps more than a hint of this danger today in what has become something of a smorgasbord 'pick and choose' approach to the faith. This is dangerous and can lead us into the subtle temptation of making God in our own image.

I experienced an extreme example of this when I visited the Martin Luther Memorial Church in Berlin to speak at a conference on reconciliation. This is one of the hundred churches that Hitler built to clothe his Nazi ideology with Christian respectability. The organ was first used in National Socialist rallies in 1935. Among the traditional nativity scene, beautifully carved in wood around the pulpit, are German soldiers. In the wooden carvings around the font, we find strong Aryan women with their strong Aryan babies and a Nazi storm trooper. The Christ on the cross behind the altar is muscular and unflinching. The message is clear: there is no suffering here. In the stone archway around the east end are carved crosses and, among them, soldiers and, until recently – when they became illegal – swastikas. Hitler, of course, is not by a long measure the only national leader to have cloaked toxic, indeed evil, policy in a Christian guise. God makes humanity in the image of God but we humans so readily make God in our own image. Hitler is an extreme example of this, but it would surely be rash not to recognise, lurking within each of us, a tendency to prefer a Christ who agrees with us to the Christ who calls and challenges us to change and to go on being changed.

To let God be real for us, in us and through us, we need again and again to return to God and to the word of God. This means submission and obedience to God. Obedience means listening, trusting and doing what God says. This is cruciformity in action. The word 'obedience', like the word 'repentance', may not play well to many today. It may have connotations of domination, oppression or even slavery. But just as repentance understood in a Christian context is actually the doorway to joy, so freely chosen obedience to Christ is the doorway to freedom. As Paul writes, 'For freedom Christ has set us free' (Galatians 5:1). Eugene Peterson, borrowing a phrase from Nietzsche, describes Christian discipleship as 'a long obedience in the same direction'.[25] What is the nature of this obedience? There is an important clue to this in the etymology of the word, both in the English (*ob-audire*) and in the Greek (*hypakoe*). In each language, the root of the word means 'to listen' or 'to hear'. Obedience is about listening to the word of God, hearing it and responding to it. Just as God's love is not coercive and is freely given, so the response of obedience must be *freely* chosen.

When I take our dogs for a walk and let them off the lead to explore, most of the time they are obedient. That is to say, they come when they are called. Except, that is, when they have seen or scented a squirrel or a rabbit. When this happens, they practise a kind of selective deafness. They edit out what they do not want to hear because what they are doing is so much more fun, or so they believe – forgive the anthropomorphism – than listening to my calls and obeying. What they don't know is that the reason I am calling them back is because I love them (dog lovers will understand) and I don't want them to chase a rabbit over the road and get run over. In their selective deafness, they choose not to hear and obey their master's voice. Like them, we too practise selective deafness not only with others but also with God. As Mark Twain said, 'It ain't the parts of the Bible I don't understand that bother me, it's the parts that I do.'

Our obedience is daring to trust that what God wants for us is infinitely better than anything that comes from 'the devices and desires of our own hearts'. It is in this obedience, counter-intuitive though it may seem, and countercultural though it may be, that we discover an inner freedom that our egotistical choices will never give us.

———— ◆ ————

Pause to ponder

Jesus answered him, 'Those who love me will keep my word, and my Father will love them, and we will come to them and will make our home with them.'
JOHN 14:23

Pause for prayer

Blessed… are those who hear the word of God and obey it!
LUKE 11:28

O Lord, the light of the minds that know you,
the joy of the hearts that love you,
and the strength of the wills that serve you:
grant us so to know you
that we may truly love you,
so to love you that we may freely serve you,
whom to serve is perfect freedom.
St Augustine of Hippo[26]

———— ◆ ————

Jesus' question to us: 'For what will it profit [you] if [you] gain the whole world but forfeit [your] life?' (Matthew 16:26).

Ceramic of Asian Christ

God so loved the world that he gave his only Son, so that
everyone who believes in him may not perish but may have
eternal life.

JOHN 3:16

6

Turned by love: 'the love that moves the sun and the stars'[1]

The immense love of God

The motive for the existence of the world and for the coming of Christ to the world are the same: the manifesting of the immense love of God.

St Isaac the Syrian[2]

A *Geronda* – or Spiritual Elder – a man of profound humility and luminosity whom I had the privilege to meet on Mount Athos, said to me, 'The greatest heresy in the church today is lack of love.'[3] A church – and any manifestation of its witness – that is not inspired and animated by the love of God in Christ is a denial of its own raison d'être. Whatever demonstrations of spiritual prowess, measures of success or examples of self-sacrifice that may issue from such a church – or indeed such a Christian – without love are worth nothing. Is not this the point Paul makes so eloquently in 1 Corinthians 13?

> If I speak in the tongues of mortals and of angels, but do not have love, I am a noisy gong or a clanging cymbal. And if I have prophetic powers, and understand all mysteries and all knowledge, and if I have all faith, so as to remove mountains, but do not have love, I am nothing. If I give away all my possessions, and if I hand over my body so that I may boast, but do not have love, I gain nothing.

1 CORINTHIANS 13:1–3

In an age when we may be in danger of thinking we need to prove ourselves, even, if we are not careful, as one ideology in the marketplace competing against others, or when we are tempted to justify ourselves simply with measurements recognised by the world, these words are salutary. Why? Because, as John of the Cross writes, 'At the evening of life, we shall be judged on our love.'[4] As Christians, above all we are to beware of seeking our approval ratings from others before God (John 5:44; 12:43; Galatians 1:10). T.S. Eliot writes in 'Little Gidding' of the salutary reflections of age, and the discomforting recognition of our past self-deceptions and lives lived for the approval of others.

> *And last, the rending pain of re-enactment*
> *Of all that you have done and been; the shame*
> *Of motives late revealed and the awareness*
> *Of things ill done and done to others harm*
> *Which once you took for exercise of virtue.*
> *Then fools' approval stings and honour stains.*[5]

Human approval is a dangerous goal, public recognition an insidious priority. Perhaps if we truly knew the love of God, we would not feel the need to seek them.

Treasure, hidden in a field

There is something important here about the hiddenness of the kingdom of God: something about the tiny, almost invisible, mustard seed relative to the huge and majestic cedar of Lebanon. There is something about the way God works, so often unseen or unnoticed, beneath the radar of public news, away from the limelight of media or social media. The kingdom of God, Jesus says, is like treasure hidden in a field. I remember well walking on the island of Mull and, a long way from any path, coming across some of the most beautiful lilies I have ever seen growing entirely away from the gaze and appreciation of humanity. But, I wondered, was the fact that their beauty would hardly ever be seen by people important? Apparently not to God, I thought. I thought of the whole creation praising God, as in the *Benedicite*, 'Praise the Lord all created things, sing his praise and exalt him forever', and Francis of Assisi's 'Canticle of the sun', where all creation praises God irrespective of human involvement. 'Nothing that he has made,' writes Francis de Sales, 'is not filled with the praise of God.'[6] I thought of the hiddenness to humanity of so much that is important to God.

It made me think about Charles de Foucauld, in Algeria, whose life and witness were hidden and intentionally so. In his love and prayer, he served local Muslims with such humility. He was murdered and, to some Christians, his life seemed at the time such a waste, a hidden life with no immediate visible fruit. But in the case of Charles de Foucauld, the fruitfulness of his ministry was in direct proportion to the hiddenness of his ministry. He died before the fruits of his faithfulness were seen. The Little Brothers of Jesus and, later, The Little Sisters of Jesus, were born and inspired by Charles de Foucauld to witness to God's special love for the poorest of the poor all over the world. This hidden witness of prayer and service continues today.

On a personal note, I think also of a deeply saintly woman, Mabel, unknown to almost everybody, who was housebound, living high up in a tower block of flats in an inner-city parish in which I served. She, in her great humility and prayerfulness, radiated the love of Christ. When I and other clergy met with her, we knew we were on holy ground. On her little balcony, she had stocks growing in her flower pots. Extraordinarily, they were in bloom not only from spring to summer but remained in flower into the autumn and even into the winter. (To which a friend of mine remarked, 'If you think that's a coincidence, have a boring day!') Mabel's life was hidden. Like those hidden lilies, but so much more, her life glorified God. It is so often out of the limelight of public life and even of visible church life that God is glorified. The value of our lives and ministries to God will likely bear little resemblance to their estimation in the marketplace. Jesus makes plain that almost everything about our inner life and relationship with God must be expressed outside the public eye, whether it be our giving (Matthew 6:3), our praying (Matthew 6:5) or our fasting (Matthew 6:18). God sees us in secret.

I remember being in hospital some 25 years ago, in a quite serious condition, when I was approached by a consultant, surrounded by a large number of other trainee doctors in white coats. This was a powerful display of the hierarchy of medicine, where the most qualified, indicated by their uniform, appeared to give what their professionalism could give. Unsurprisingly, I felt that they were observing me not so much as a human being or one of them, but more as a 'condition' or a 'case' to be solved. With due and very genuine gratitude for the advances of medical science that they represented and on which I depended, something very important was missing; the expression of common humanity. No doubt the professional medical assessment and resulting prescription were important, but what I felt to be most helpful to my inner well-being, to how I *felt*, was contributed by the humanising banter of the hospital porters and the chat with those who came with food and the drinks trolley. This was all away from and unnoticed by those who saw themselves at the apex of the medical hierarchy of healing. In this context, it is interesting to note that the World Health Organisation describes the most important ingredient in the healing that takes place in hospitals as 'atmosphere'.

God so often works subliminally in ways that are hidden, outside the values of the world and, when seen, surprising to the eyes of the world. In the parable of the sheep and the goats (Matthew 25:31–46), the dominant note is one of surprise. Some assumed their lives were pleasing to God; others did not dare presume such a thing. Each group was surprised by God's response, asking, 'When did we do this? When did we not do that?'

———— ◆ ————

Pause to ponder

In our missional engagements, it is surely true that others will be drawn to Christ only if they sense the presence of his love in us and through us.

> Mission is the extension of the love of the Trinitarian God, for the transformation in love of the whole world.
> Archbishop Anastasios of Albania[7]

> We are not called by God to do extraordinary things, but to do ordinary things with love.
> Jean Vanier[8]

Pause for prayer

> Keep me as the apple of your eye; hide me in the shadow of your wings.
> PSALM 17:8 (NIV)

Help us, Lord, to do the ordinary things of this day with love.

'How few of his disciples really love him'[9]

One of the most helpful spiritual exercises we can do is to allow Jesus to ask us the questions he asks others in the gospels and to spend time with him discerning and articulating what our honest answer actually is to each of these questions. This honest dialogue with God can help revive flagging faith and be profoundly life giving. Among such important questions are:

> Why are you afraid, you of little faith?
> MATTHEW 8:26

What do you want me to do for you?
MARK 10:51

Do you want to be made well?
JOHN 5:6

Who do you say that I am?
MATTHEW 16:15

Do you love me?
JOHN 21:17

Each of these questions deserves proper time for pondering and then for dialogue with God and prayer. They are not questions seeking speculative or analytical answers. They are existential questions addressed to our hearts. We might want to stay with that last question, addressed to Peter – 'Do you love me?' – and to take time out, even now if appropriate, to ponder it in a quiet time with God.

It may well be that our honest answer to that question depends, to a degree at least, on how far we have apprehended, discovered, trusted or experienced the love of God for us. It may be something that we know *about*, because we have heard about it from others and read about it in the scriptures. It may be that at some quite deep level we don't actually believe ourselves to be truly lovable. How could God love me if he knows what I am truly like? Or it may be a diffident and godly humility that holds us back. As the priest-poet George Herbert puts it, 'Love bade me welcome: yet my soul drew back, guilty of dust and sin.'[10] We find it hard to believe that God could truly love us so passionately. The poet, who in dialogue with God describes himself as 'I, the unkind, the ungrateful', discovers that God loves him as he is and that God, or Love, 'bore the blame'. It was this poem, inviting a response to God's love, that changed the life of Simone Weil. She writes, 'I used to think I was merely reciting it as a beautiful poem, but without my knowing it, the recitation had the virtue of a prayer. It was during one of these recitations that Christ came down and took possession of me.'[11] Dare we allow ourselves to believe and trust this invitation of love?

'We love because he first loved us'

Herbert's poem 'Love' evokes something of the love that *woos* us, as Hosea describes: 'But now I am going to woo her – I will bring her out to the desert and I will speak to her heart' (Hosea 2:14, CJB). It evokes God, who as a shepherd, is out *searching* for us – 'I myself will search for my sheep, and will seek them out' (Ezekiel 34:11) – searching in love for that one lost sheep which is you or me (Luke 15:3–7). It points to the God who will not stop searching for us, evoked so vividly in the poem 'The Hound of Heaven' by Francis Thompson.

If we are searching for God, it is a response to God's searching for us. St John of the Cross writes, 'In the first place it should be known that if anyone is seeking God, the Beloved is seeking that person much more.'[12] If we are searching for God, it is a sign that God is already in us and that God has already found us. It may be that we have never thought of God in these terms. We have thought only of our longing for God and never of God's longing for us. We have never imagined that, as Gregory of Nazianzus puts it, 'God thirsts to be thirsted after'[13] – or, in the words of Thérèse of Lisieux, that Christ is 'parched' for our love. She writes:

> Jesus is parched, for he meets only the ungrateful and indifferent among his own disciples, alas he finds few hearts who surrender to him without reservations, who understand the real tenderness of his infinite love.[14]

Thérèse grieves at the lack of love in the disciples of Christ. She knows, as the apostle Paul did, how we can get so caught up in doing things – even good and wonderful things – for God, and the works of the church, that we miss out the one thing that matters most: 'He has no need of our works, only of our love.'[15] Centuries earlier, Teresa of Ávila, who knew the intimacy of God's love, wrote, 'Our Lord does not care so much for the importance of our works as for the love with which they are done.'[16] There is a poignant Rupnik mosaic of Francis of Assisi, on his own, weeping in the woods, lamenting that 'God is not loved enough', 'Love is not loved.'[17] St Mary Magdalene de Pazzi (1566–1607) shares in the same lament. In 1583, her Carmelite sisters saw her weeping before the crucifix and crying out, 'O Love, you are not known or loved'; 'O Love, love is not loved, not known by his own creatures.'[18] The love Thérèse of Lisieux has for Jesus makes her 'long to console him for the ingratitude of the wicked'. She prays, 'O my God, most Blessed Trinity, I desire to make you loved.'[19] Truly, to know the love of God is to long for God to be loved more. But, of course, love cannot compel love or it would not be love. Love can only invite love.

So what might be the barriers within us or around us that prevent us experiencing or trusting this love and then responding to it? One of them might be that we have become a bit stuck or stunted at an early stage of Christian development. Augustine of Hippo tells the story of a young couple deeply in love. The young man gives her the most beautiful ring in the world. As she becomes more and more entranced and mesmerised by the ring, gradually her attention moves from the giver to the gift. This is akin to what Bernard of Clairvaux describes as the second stage (out of four) of Christian maturity, namely, loving God for what we can get out of him, or loving God because it is in our interest to do so. The third stage, according to Bernard, is loving God for *God's* sake. The anonymous author of The Cloud of Unknowing exhorts the reader several times to this very thing: 'Lift up your heart to God with humble love: and mean God himself, and not what you get out of him.'[20]

> For though it is good to think about the kindness of God, and to love and praise him for it, it is far better to think about him as he is and to love and praise him *for himself*.[21]

Question: How far do we actually love God for who God is, as distinct from what we receive from him?

Pause to ponder

You are precious in my sight, and honoured, and I love you.
ISAIAH 43:4

Truly, one who touches you touches the apple of my eye.
ZECHARIAH 2:8

The Lord, your God… will rejoice over you with gladness, he will renew you in his love; he will exult over you with loud singing.
ZEPHANIAH 3:17

Pause for prayer

My child, give me your heart.
PROVERBS 23:26

See what love the Father has given us, that we should be called children of God; and that is what we are.
1 JOHN 3:1

O my God, you know that for loving you on earth
I have only today.
St Thérèse of Lisieux[22]

Love so amazing, so divine, demands my soul, my life, my all.
Isaac Watts[23]

Another barrier might be that we are living too much in our heads, where God remains in the realm of thoughts or ideas. We do not make space for God at a deeper level, of existential encounter, where 'deep calls to deep' (Psalm 42:7). We might not be used to bringing our feelings to God. On my first individually guided retreat many years ago, after a few of our daily meetings when I would invariably begin answering questions with 'I *think*…', my guide interrupted me with 'I'm not interested in what you *think*, I want to know "What do you *feel*?"' Have we allowed a separation between head and heart, and chosen the head? At the heart of Orthodox teaching on prayer is the healing of this division; we are to pray 'with the mind in the heart'. Likewise, the author of *The Cloud of Unknowing* is clear that thinking about God will not lead us to the experience of God. Thinking about God and the goodness and love of God is good, but something more is needed and that is the act of *loving* God: 'By love he can be caught and held, but by thinking, never.'[24] Origen, reflecting on the last supper with the beloved disciple lying on the heart of Jesus, wrote that we can never truly understand John's gospel unless we can imagine ourselves lying on the heart of Jesus. For some of us, there may be inhibitions to this intimacy. We find it hard to trust our whole selves to God.

This, of course, brings us back to our primary identity, which for each of us is as a *child* of God. Jesus calls us to become as children. 'He wants us,' Mother Julian writes, 'to show a child's characteristics, which always trusts in his mother's love, in well-being and in woe.'[25] Do we know ourselves as children of God, not simply as servants of God? Can we be as children, that is to say child*like* not child*ish*, with God? Do we feel free to play, to be spontaneous? Can we allow God, as Pope Francis asks, simply to gaze on us in his love? Or has our experience or understanding of the institutional church discouraged or impeded this freedom? William Blake captures well this tension between innocence and experience in 'The Garden of Love':

> *I went to the Garden of Love,*
> *And saw what I never had seen:*
> *A Chapel was built in the midst,*
> *Where I used to play on the green.*

> *And the gates of this Chapel were shut,*
> *And Thou shalt not, writ over the door;*
> *So I turned to the Garden of Love,*
> *That so many sweet flowers bore.*
>
> *And I saw it was filled with graves,*
> *And tomb-stones where flowers should be:*
> *And Priests in black gowns, were walking their rounds,*
> *And binding with briars my joys and desires.*[26]

In the light of this, we might want to ask ourselves some questions. For example, is our religion making us more 'religious' or more *alive*? Has our, quite proper, focus on goals for the church subtly eclipsed our desire to know Christ more and to make him known?

The beauty of God

The psalmist writes, 'One thing I asked of the Lord, that will I seek after: to live in the house of the Lord all the days of my life, *to behold the beauty of the Lord*' (Psalm 27:4). The church, in the west especially, has neglected beauty both as an attribute of God and as a gateway to God. We hear and speak the language of the goodness of God and the truth of God, but we seem to have forgotten the beauty of God. In John's gospel, as William Temple points out, when Jesus says, 'I am the good shepherd' (John 10:11), the word John uses is not *agathos*, denoting moral goodness; it is *kalos*, meaning fine or beautiful. Jesus is the *beautiful* shepherd. Beauty attracts. Augustine of Hippo writes in his *Confessions*, 'Too late have I loved you, beauty so ancient and so new.'[27] The beauty of God draws us to God, who is also goodness and truth. Fyodor Dostoyevsky famously writes in his novel *The Idiot*, 'Beauty will save the world', and in a letter to a friend (Natalya Fonvizina), 'I believe nothing is more beautiful… and perfect than Christ.'[28]

In the Orthodox Church, the beauty of God is both honoured and reflected in worship. In 987 Prince Vladimir of Kiev sent emissaries to Constantinople to seek out a new religion for his people. After experiencing the Divine Liturgy there, they reported:

> We knew not whether we were in heaven or on earth. For on earth there is no such splendour or beauty and we are at a loss to describe it. We only know that God dwells there among people and their service is fairer than the ceremonies of other nations. For we cannot forget the beauty.

This beauty was the gateway to Christian faith and to the establishment of the Orthodox Church in Russian Kiev. So an Orthodox has said, 'We do not proselytise; we seduce!'

———— ◆ ————

Question: Have we in the western church majored on morality at the expense of beauty?

———— ◆ ————

In the first creation account in Genesis 1, after every act of creating, God the creator looked and 'saw that it was good'. In the culminating act of creation, the creation of humankind, God looks at all that he has made 'and indeed, it was very good' (Genesis 1:31). The Hebrew word translated 'good' can equally mean 'beautiful' and in the first Greek translation of the Old Testament, the Septuagint, once more the word used is *kalos*, meaning 'fine' or 'beautiful'. God's creation is beautiful. Humanity is made in the image of God, who is beautiful, though we have marred this beauty. God's Son is beautiful, 'the reflection of God's glory' (Hebrews 1:3). The Holy Spirit works in us to restore in us the image of his beauty. Irenaeus of Lyons describes the work of God in us when we offer ourselves to him:

His hand will gild you inside and out, with pure gold and silver, and so adorn you that the King himself will desire your beauty. If therefore you offer to him what is yours, that is faith in him and subjection, you will receive his art and become a perfect work of God.[29]

We are to let God do his work in us. We are to let God love us. Mother Julian refers to God as the sweet eye of love that never stops gazing on us. In Ignatian spiritual direction, we are encouraged to bathe or to bask in the loving gaze of God, to know ourselves, to experience ourselves as loved by God.

We do not have to change for God to love us, but to experience God's love will change us.

Pause to ponder

One thing I asked of the Lord, that will I seek after: to live in the house of the Lord all the days of my life, to behold the beauty of the Lord, and to inquire in his temple.
PSALM 27:4

Behold God beholding you… and smiling.
Anthony de Mello SJ[30]

When he gave me himself, he gave me back myself.
St Bernard of Clairvaux[31]

Too late have I loved you, Beauty so ancient and so new, late have I loved you. Lo, you were within, but I outside, seeking for you there. You were with me but I was not with you.
St Augustine of Hippo[32]

Pause for prayer

Lord, you are closer to me
than my own breathing,
nearer than my hands and feet.
St Teresa of Ávila[33]

How shall we become lovely? By loving him who is lovely.
St Augustine of Hippo[34]

———— ◆ ————

Madly in love with us

Catherine of Siena begins one of her prayers with the words 'Eternal Trinity, you who are madly in love with your creatures'.[35] God's love is both universal and deeply personal. It is, at one and the same time, both the love that moves the sun and the stars, as Dante puts it, and it is also the love that calls each of us by name.

I have been much inspired by a visit to Pennyhooks Care Farm. It is an organic farm, which respects creation as a gift to be honoured and nurtured. It is also, inspiringly, where young people and adults with autism spectrum condition work. Each person is recognised as unique in character, personality and gifts, and in the particular challenges they face with their autism. Those who run the farm, Lydia and Richard, in their expertise and care discern exactly which farm work and which animals will bring out the best of what each young person can offer and give, as each one of them makes a unique contribution to the success of the farm and to the community of which they are a part. Each young person is, quite literally, called by name in every conversation. The respect and affirmation they receive, like God's love, is personal. We might even describe this love as 'bespoke' in that it is tailored to the unique particularities of each person.

Jesus tells the disciples, 'Even the hairs of your head are all counted' (Matthew 10:30). To be known, loved and called by name, of course, brings out the best in each person, in each of us. We *respond* to such love, and each of us does so uniquely. When I receive birthday cards from my daughters, each of them in the choice of the card, in what they say in it and in the way they say it will be expressing something uniquely and personally.

As sisters and brothers for whom Christ died, each of us is known, loved and called by name. God's love for us is passionate and deeply costly. God longs for a response. Though it may sound hackneyed, his RSVP is written in the blood of Christ shed on the cross. It is not enough simply to acknowledge it or to receive like some spiritual couch potato, or as the *consumers* our western cultures have encouraged us to be. We are called to *respond* to this love and to do so wholeheartedly.

Clare of Assisi writes, 'Love him totally, who gave himself totally for your love.' When we respond to the love of God with our love, Clare writes, 'We become what we love and who we love shapes what we become.'[36] Gregory of Nyssa writes, 'When we turn to God we become that which he is himself.'[37] This is because it is the movement of the Spirit in us that draws us to God, the holy Trinity. It is God's love for us that evokes our love for God. It is always God's grace, always God's initiative. We love him because he first loved us. Jeremiah knows that he and we need God first to turn us to God: 'Turn me and I shall be turned, for you are the Lord my God' (Jeremiah 31:18, GW). The psalmist implores, three times, 'Turn us again, O God, and cause thy face to shine; and we shall be saved' (Psalm 80:3, 7, 19, KJV). Without God, we can do nothing. John Donne (1572–1631), poet and Dean of St Paul's, recognising his helplessness without God, in the language of erotic desire, urges God to:

> *Take me to you, imprison me, for I,*
> *Except you enthral me, never shall be free,*
> *Nor ever chaste, except you ravish me.*[38]

God creates us in love; he comes to meet us in Christ as love; and through the Holy Spirit, we are recreated in love. To begin to glimpse, to apprehend, to experience this love and the *cost* of this loving – which 'my God feels as blood; but I, as wine'[39] – is for love to be awakened in ourselves. This, so much more than being a duty, is a joy, a joyful adventure. Like Abram and Sarai, we set out in faith not knowing where God will lead us. We cannot dictate or domesticate the movements of the Holy Spirit. As Jesus tells Nicodemus, 'The wind blows where it chooses, and you hear the sound of it, but you do not know where it comes from or where it is goes. So it is with everyone who is born of the Spirit' (John 3:8).

This adventure is, in the words of Father Joseph P. Whelan SJ (1907–91), worth getting out of bed for:

> *Nothing is more practical than finding God,*
> *Than falling in Love in a quite absolute, final way.*
> *What you are in love with,*
> *what seizes your imagination,*
> *will affect everything.*
> *It will decide what will get you out of bed in the morning,*
> *what you do with your evenings,*
> *how you spend your weekends,*
> *what you read,*
> *whom you know,*
> *what breaks your heart,*
> *and what amazes you with joy and gratitude.*
> *Fall in Love, stay in love,*
> *and it will decide everything.*[40]

The good news of the gospel is that we can start again now, as forgiven sinners, as ones called by name and as ones sent to witness to his love. Whatever our thoughts about this, thinking alone will not be enough. This is about a decision. It is about choosing life. The words of scripture, God-breathed, are for us here and now. They are of course historical, first spoken by Jesus at a particular time and place. They are also always present tense; that is, they are for each and all of us *now*, this very moment.

Jesus says, 'The time is fulfilled, and the kingdom of God has come near; repent, and believe the good news' (Mark 1:15).

Jesus' question to us: 'Do you love me?'

Thérèse of Lisieux puts it so simply, 'O my God, you know that for loving you on earth I have only today.'[41]

Illustrations

Cover and page 30: Pastor Dr P. Solomon Raj, *The Return* (1987). Batik.
Copyright: All works by Solomon Raj reproduced by permission of his son, Pulidindi Augustine Jyothi Raj.

Page 12: *Moses in Front of the Burning Bush* (12th/13th century). Loca sancta icon. St Catherine's Monastery (Sinai, Egypt).
Copyright: Painting is in the public domain because of its age.
Photograph copyright: Jim Forest.

Page 15: Stanley Spencer, *Christ in the Wilderness: Consider the lilies* (1939). Oil on canvas (56 x 56 cm), State Art Collection, Art Gallery of Western Australia. Purchased 1983.
Copyright: Reproduced by permission.

Page 28: Iconographic workshop of Bose Monastery (Italy), *St Anne*. Fasas Cathedral (Egypt). Egg tempera on wood.
Copyright: Reproduced by permission of Bose Monastery.

Page 48: Iconographic workshop of Bose Monastery (Italy), *The Foot-Washing of Christ of the Disciples*. Byzantine style. Egg tempera on board.
Copyright: Reproduced by permission of Bose Monastery.

Pages 68 and 82: Pastor Dr P. Solomon Raj, *The Sending* (1987). Batik.
Copyright: As per cover.

Page 69: Sister Lara Sacco, *The Virgin of the Sign* (2018). Bose
Monastery (Italy).
Copyright: Reproduced by permission.

Page 73: Iconographic workshop of the Bose Monastery (Italy), *The
Hospitality of Abraham and Sarah*. Coptic style. Egg tempera on
board.
Copyright: Reproduced by permission of Bose Monastery.

Page 74: Andrei Rublev, *The Trinity* (1425).
Copyright: Painting is in the public domain because of its age.

Page 78: Pastor Dr P. Solomon Raj, *Behind the Barbed Wire* (1986).
Woodcut.
Copyright: As per cover.

Page 90: Pastor Dr P. Solomon Raj, *Evangelism and Mercy* (1982).
Batik.
Copyright: As per cover.

Page 101: Detail from the Parvis of Ta' Pinu National Shrine (2017)
by the Centro Aletti, led by Father Marko Rupnik SJ. These
'Mysteries of the Rosary' are on the shrine in Gozo (Malta).
Copyright: Reproduced by permission.

Page 110: This icon with the Asian Christ was gifted to the
Benedictine monastery of Rostrevor, County Down, Northern
Ireland.
Copyright: Reproduced by permission of the Holy Cross
Monastery.

Notes

Chapter 1   Turning aside: to look and to see

1 Holy Transfiguration Monastery (tr.), *The Ascetical Homilies of Saint Isaac the Syrian* (Holy Transfiguration Monastery, 2011), p. 467.

2 St Ignatius of Antioch, *The Epistle to The Ephesians*.

3 Evelyn Underhill, *The Spiritual Life* (Morehouse Publishing, 2008), p. 20.

4 St Augustine of Hippo, *Confessions*, book X, chapter XXVII.

5 Meister Eckhart, *Mysticism*, chapter 6.

6 R.S. Thomas, *Collected Poems: 1945–1990* (Phoenix, 2004), p. 302. Used by permission.

7 Kallistos Ware, *The Power of the Name* (accessed via **oodegr.com/ english/psyxotherap/dyn_onom1.htm**)

8 William H. Davies, *Collected Poems* (Alfred A. Knopf, 1916) p. 18.

9 Ronald de Leeuw (ed.), *The Letters of Vincent van Gogh* (Penguin Books, 1997), p. 6.

10 Elizabeth Barrett Browning (ed. Kerry McSweeney), *Aurora Leigh* (Oxford University Press, 2008), p. 246.

11 Thomas, *Collected poems*, p. 302. Used by permission.

12 G.M. Hopkins, *Poems and Prose* (Penguin, 1985), p. 27.

13 Esther de Waal, *Seeking God* (Fount, 1984), p. 65.

14 St Neilus of Ankara, *Exhortation to Monks*, paragraph 79, 1236B.

15 Mother Julian of Norwich, *Showings*, chapter 22.

16 Robert Llewelyn (ed.), *The Joy of the Saints* (Darton, Longman and Todd, 1988), p. 4.

17 William Blake, *The Marriage of Heaven and Hell* (Dover Publications, 1994), p. 36.

18 T.S. Eliot, *Collected Poems 1909–62* (Faber and Faber Ltd, 1974), p. 178. Used by permission.

19 W.H. Auden, *Collected Poems* (Faber and Faber Limited, 1994), p. 533. Reprinted by permission of Curtis Brown, Ltd.

20 Joseph Conrad, *Lord Jim* (Penguin, 2007), p. 63.

21 Auden, *Collected Poems*, p. 249. Reprinted by permission of Curtis Brown, Ltd.

22 Basil Hume, *The Intentional Life* (Paraclete Press, 2003), p. 22.

23 Blaise Pascal (tr. A.J. Krailshimer), *Pensées* (Penguin Books, 1966), p. 67.

24 John Greenleaf Whittier, 'Dear Lord and Father of mankind' (1872).

Chapter 2   Turning to Christ: repentance

1   St John Climacus (tr. Archimandrite Lazarus Moore), *The Ladder of Divine Ascent* (Harper & Brothers, 1959), p. 49.

2   Aleksandr Solzhenitsyn, *The Gulag Archipelago 1918–1956* (Harvill Press, 2003), p. 312.

3   Quoted by Robert Llewelyn, *The Joy of the Saints* (Darton, Longman and Todd, 1988), p. 254.

4   Simone Weil, *Waiting for God* (Putnam, 1951; reprint 2009), p. 7.

5   William Shakespeare, *Measure for Measure*, Act II, Scene II.

6   John Chrysostom (ed. S. Zincone), *Homilies on the Gospel of Saint Matthew* (Rome, 2003), p. 371.

7   Holy Transfiguration Monastery (tr.), *The Ascetical Homilies of Saint Isaac the Syrian* (Holy Transfiguration Monastery, 2011), p. 387.

8   *The Ascetical Homilies of Saint Isaac the Syrian*, p. 387.

9   John Wesley, *The Principles of a Methodist Farther Explain'd* (W. Strahan, 1746), p. 69.

10 John Griffiths (ed.), *Book of Homilies* (Regent College Publishing, 2008), p. 525.

11 St John Climacus, *The Ladder of Divine Ascent*, p. 29.

12 *The Ascetical Homilies of Saint Isaac the Syrian*, p. 357.

13 Quoted by Arthur Skevington Wood (ed.), *Gift of Love: Daily readings (Enfolded in love)* (Darton, Longman and Todd, 1987), p. xii.

14 Quoted by Wood, *Gift of Love*, p. x.

15 Quoted in Pseudo-Macarius (tr. George A. Maloney), *The Fifty Spiritual Homilies and the Great Letter* (Paulist Press, 1992), p. xi.

16 Quoted in Pseudo-Macarius, *The Fifty Spiritual Homilies*, p. 89.

17 Richard Hooker, *Laws of Ecclesiastical Polity*, in John Keble (ed.), *Works* (At the Clarendon Press, 1876), p. 200. Accessed via **anglicanhistory.org/hooker/5/5.200-209.pdf**.

18 Mother Julian of Norwich, *Revelations of Divine Love*, chapter 52.

19 Pope John XXIII, *Journal of a Soul* (Geoffrey Chapman, 2000), p. 450.

20 Henry Bull, *Prayer and Meditations* (Parker Society, 1842), p. xix.

21 Quoted in *Bulletin of Spiritual Edification*, 10 March 2013. Ecumenical Patriarchate. Archdiocese of Thyateira and Great Britain.

22 H.G.C. Moule, *Charles Simeon* (Inter-Varsity Press, 1956), pp. 133–34.

23 'The Revival' by Henry Vaughan (1621–95), accessed via **bartleby. com/library/poem/5403.html**.

24 Mother Julian of Norwich, *Revelations of Divine Love*, chapter 72.

25 Anonymous, *The Cloud of Unknowing* (Penguin, 1982), p. 100.

26 Elder Paisios of Mount Athos, *Epistles* (Holy Monastery of the Evangelist John the Theologian, 2002), p. 150.

27 'To a Louse' in James Barke (ed.), *Poems and Songs of Robert Burns* (Fletcher & Son, 1977), p. 138.

28 Archimandrite Aimilianos of Simonopetra, *The Way of the Spirit* (Indeiktos, 2009), pp. 25–26.

29 Dorotheus of Gaza, *Discourses and Sayings* (Cistercian Publications, 2008), p. 98.

30 Jean-Pierre De Caussade, *Abandonment to Divine Providence* (Catholic Way Publishing, 2013), p. 406.

31 St Francis de Sales, *Introduction to the Devout Life* (Catholic Way Publishing 2015), p. 20.

32 Thomas Merton, *Conjectures of a Guilty Bystander* (Sheldon Press, 1977), p. 93.

33 Quoted by Llewelyn, *The Joy of the Saints*, p. 197.

34 Benedicta Ward (tr.), *Prayers and Meditations of St Anselm* (Penguin, 1973), pp. 93–94.

35 Thomas Traherne, *Centuries of Meditations* (Cosimo, 2007), Cent. 51, Cent. 45.

36 St Augustine of Hippo, *Confessions*, Book I, chapter I.

37 Quoted by Robert Atwell, *Celebrating the Saints* (SCM Press, 2004), p. 319.

38 St Gregory of Nazianzus (ed. Verna E.F. Harrison), *Festal Orations* (SVS Press, 2008), p. 123.

39 Quoted in Simon Tugwell OP, *Ways of Imperfection* (Templegate, 1985), p. 98.

40 Ward, *Prayers and Meditations of St Anselm*, pp. 93–94.

Chapter 3   Turning in love: for one another

1 Tertullian, *Apologeticum*, chapter 39:7.

2 Tertullian, *Apologeticum*, chapter 50:13.

3 Teresa of Ávila, *The Way of Perfection* (Sheed and Ward, 1999), p. 157.

4 Lesslie Newbigin, *The Gospel in a Pluralist Society* (Eerdmans, 1989), p. 227.

5 Dorotheus of Gaza, *On Refusal to Judge our Neighbour*, Instruction VI.

6 Michael Ramsey, address given to the Fellowship of St Alban and St Sergius, 1960.

7 Quoted by Kallistos of Diokleia at XXIII International Ecumenical Convention on Orthodox Spirituality, Mercy and Forgiveness, Bose, September 2015.

8 Dietrich Bonhoeffer, *Life Together* (Harper, 2008), p. 86.

9 Quoted in Brennan Manning, *Ragamuffin Gospel* (Multnomah Books, 2005), p. 25.

10 St Aristides, *Apology*, chapter 16.

11 Kallistos of Diokleia at XXIII International Ecumenical Convention.

12 Eric P. Wheeler, *Dorotheos of Gaza: Discourses and sayings* (Cistercian Publications, 1977), p. 219.

13 Leo Tolstoy, *Anna Karenina* (Penguin Books Ltd, 2006), p. 418.

14 Holy Transfiguration Monastery (tr.), *The Ascetical Homilies of Saint Isaac the Syrian* (Holy Transfiguration Monastery, 2011), p. 64.

15 John Behr, *Asceticism and Anthropology in Irenaeus and Clement* (Oxford University Press, 2007), p. 117.

16 Quoted in Robert Llewelyn, *Our Duty and Our Joy* (Darton, Longman and Todd, 1993), p. 6.

17 George Herbert, 'King of Glory, King of Peace' (1633).

18 Anonymous, *The Cloud of Unknowing* (Penguin, 1982), p. 61.

19 George Herbert, *The Complete English Poems* (Penguin, 2004), pp. 115–16.

20 Behr, *Asceticism and Anthropology*, p. 117.

21 Bonhoeffer, *Life Together*, p. 15.

22 Samuel Taylor Coleridge, *Aids to Reflection*, 'Moral and religious aphorisms', Aphorism 25.

23 Søren Kierkegaard (ed. Alastair Hannay), *Papers and Journals: A selection* (Penguin, 1996), p. 609.

24 *The Cloud of Unknowing*, p. 60.

25 I read this on a leaflet at the Wantage community many years ago.

26 *The Cloud of Unknowing*, p. 60.

27 George MacDonald, *Unspoken Sermons: Second series* (Cosimo, 2007), p. 211.

28 *The Rule of St Benedict* (Ampleforth Abbey Press, 1997), chapter 53.

29 Paul Tillich, *The Shaking of the Foundations* (Scribner's, 1948), pp. 161–62.

30 G.M. Hopkins, *Poems and Prose* (Penguin, 1985), p. 51.

Chapter 4 Turning outwards: in love to God's world

1 'On Love of the Poor', quoted in Olivier Clement, *The Roots of Christian Mysticism* (New City, 1993), p. 295.

2 Olivier Clément, *On Human Being* (New City, 2000), p. 37.

3 F. Brown, S. Driver and C. Briggs, *The Brown-Driver-Briggs Hebrew and English Lexicon* (Hendrickson, 1991).

4 Miroslav Volf, 'A theology of embrace for a world of exclusion' in *Explorations in Reconciliation* (Ashgate, 2006), p. 27.

5 Colin E. Gunton, *The Actuality of Atonement* (T&T Clark, 1988), p. 182.

6 John Chrysostom, 'Second letter to the Corinthians, Homily 13.1–2', in *From the Fathers to the Churches* (Collins, 1983), p. 213.

7 Martin Smith (ed.), *Benson of Cowley* (Oxford University Press, 1980), p. 107.

8 John Paul II, 'Address to the Symposium of the Council of the European Bishops' Conference', 11 October 1985.

9 This quote is often attributed to Richard Hooker, although the source is uncertain.

10 Julian the Apostate, *Letters* (1923), *Works*, vol. 3, pp. 2–235, letter 22, accessed via **tertullian.org/fathers/julian_apostate_letters_1_trans.htm**.

11 Teresa of Ávila, *The Way of Perfection* (Sheed and Ward, 1999), p. 85.

12 World Council of Churches, 'Christian unity for peace', accessed via **archive.wfn.org/2004/01/msg00169.html**.

13 John Donne, *Devotions upon Emergent Occasions* (Vintage, 1999), p. 103.

14 St Gregory of Nyssa, *That There Are Not Three Gods*, pp. 45, 117.

15 Quoted in Alexis Torrance, *Individuality in Late Antiquity* (Routledge, 2016), p. 114.

16 Derwas Chitty (ed.), *Letters of St Anthony the Great* (SLG Press, 1975), pp. 20–21.

17 William Tyndale, *Love's Redeeming Work* (Oxford University Press, 2003), p. 36.

18 Matthew Arnold (ed. J. Dover Wilson), *Culture and Anarchy: An essay in political and social criticism* (Cambridge University Press, 1932), p. 4.

19 Archimandrite Sophrony, *St Silouan the Athonite* (St Vladimir's Seminary Press, 1999), p. 371.

20 Kallistos of Diokleia, *Salvation According to St Silouan* (Sobornost 19.1), p. 46.

21 Account by Reverend H. Stirling Gahan on the Execution of Edith Cavell. *Source Records of the Great War*, Vol. III, ed. Charles F. Horne, *National Alumni 1923*, accessed via **firstworldwar.com/source/ cavell_gahan.htm**.

22 Chris Moorey, *Crowns of Barbed Wire* (CreateSpace Independent Publishing Platform, 2014), p. 123.

23 Quoted in Paul Harris (ed.), *The Fire of Silence and Stillness* (Darton, Longman and Todd, 1995), p. 17.

24 John Milton, *Areopagitica*, p. 18, accessed via **archive.org/stream/ areopagitica01miltgoog#page/n70/mode/2up/search/sallies**.

25 Simon Tugwell, *Ways of Imperfection* (Templegate, 1985), p. 134.

26 Quoted in Dietrich Bonhoeffer, *Life Together* (Harper, 2008), pp. 17–18.

27 Sophrony, *St Silouan the Athonite*, p. 114.

28 Rosemary Edmonds (tr.), *Saint Silouan the Athonite* (Patriarchal and Stavropegic Monastery of St John the Baptist, 1991), p. 352.

29 St Nikolaj Velimirović, 'Prayers by the Lake LXXV', in Bishop Artemije (ed.), *Treasures New and Old: Writings about St Nikolai Velimirovich* (Sebastien Press, 2010), p. 165.

30 The Very Reverend Richard Howard, Provost of Coventry, Christmas Day Sermon on the BBC, 1940.

31 The Spiritual Testament of Dom Christian Marie de Chergé.

32 Jon Stallworthy (ed.), *The Poems of Wilfred Owen* (Chatto and Windus, 1990), p. 126.

33 Charles Edwin Markham, 'Outwitted' in *The Shoes of Happiness and Other Poems*, accessed via **theotherpages.org/poems/mark01.html**.

34 Hans Urs von Balthasar, *Dare We Hope That All Men Be Saved?* (Ignatius Press, 2014), p. 38.

Chapter 5   Turning to the cross

1 Hans Urs von Balthasar, *Unless You Become Like This Child* (Ignatius Press 1992), p. 57.

2 Rainer Maria Rilke (tr. Robert Bly), *Selected Poems* (Harper Perennial, 1981), p. 141.

3 Dietrich Bonhoeffer, *The Cost of Discipleship* (SCM, 1959), p. 79.

4 Michael Ramsey, *The Christian Priest Today* (SPCK, 1972), p. 90 (my italics).

5 Archbishop Anastasios, *Mission in Christ's Way* (WCC Publications, 2010), p. 152.

6 Mother Julian of Norwich, *Revelations of Divine Love*, chapter 68.
7 Kosuke Koyama, *No Handle on the Cross* (SCM-Canterbury Press, 1976), p. 29.
8 Quoted in Richard Rohr, *Adam's Return* (The Crossroad Publishing Company, 2004) p. 69.
9 Sebastian Brock (tr.), *The Wisdom of Saint Isaac the Syrian* (SLG Press Convent of the Incarnation, 1997), p. 15.
10 Jean Vanier, *Drawn into the Mystery of Jesus through the Gospel of John* (Darton, Longman and Todd, 2004), p. 301.
11 Quoted in Benedicta Ward, *The Sayings of the Desert Fathers* (Mowbrays, 1983), p. 90.
12 Bonhoeffer, *The Cost of Discipleship*, p. 44.
13 W.H. Auden, *Collected Poems* (Faber and Faber Limited, 1994), p. 353. Reprinted by permission of Curtis Brown, Ltd.
14 Chandran Devanesen, 'O tree of Calvary', reproduced by kind permission of Dr Dayalan Devanesen.
15 C.S. Lewis, *The Magician's Nephew* (Harper Collins, 2001), p. 160.
16 Lewis, *The Magician's Nephew*, p. 169.
17 John Henry Newman, 'Lead, kindly light' (1833).
18 Quoted in M. Greene and C. Butcher, *The Servant Queen and the King She Serves* (The Bible Society, 2016), pp. 10–11.
19 The mosaics are made by the Centro Aletti led by Father Marko Rupnik SJ. These 'Mysteries of the Rosary' are on the Parvis of Ta' Pinu National Shrine, Gozo (Malta).
20 Quoted in Robert Llewelyn, *Our Duty and Our Joy* (Darton, Longman and Todd, 1993), p. 22.
21 George Matheson, 'O love that wilt not let me go' (1882).
22 Quoted in R.C. Sproul, *Developing Christian Character Study Guide* (Ligonier Ministries, 1998), p. 67.
23 Quoted in Thomas Keating, *Fruits and Gifts of the Spirit* (Lantern Books, 2007), p. 1.
24 *St Benedict's Rule* (Ampleforth Abbey Press, 1997), p. 6.
25 Eugene Peterson, *A Long Obedience in the Same Direction: Discipleship in an instant society*, 20th anniversary edition (IVP, 2000).
26 Quoted in Olivia Warburton, *Hear our Prayer* (Lion, 2005), p. 15.

Chapter 6   Turned by love: 'the love that moves the sun and stars'

1   Dante, *The Divine Comedy* 3, Paradise, Canto xxxiii, l.145 (Penguin Classics, 1991), p. 347.

2   St Isaac the Syrian, *Chapters on Knowledge*, IV, 79.

3   For those who might quibble with this use of the word 'heresy', usually used to describe a belief or opinion at variance with accepted orthodoxy, he might have answered that it is the love of God, the holy Trinity, that is the premise and foundational content of all Christian doctrine.

4   *Catechism of the Catholic Church* (Burns & Oates, 2000), p. 233.

5   T.S. Eliot, *Collected Poems 1909–1962* (Faber and Faber Ltd, 1974), p. 205. Used by permission.

6   Francis de Sales, *Introduction to the Devout Life* (SPCK, 2017), p. 71.

7   Archbishop Anastasios, *Mission in Christ's Way* (Holy Cross Orthodox Press, 2010), p. 221.

8   Quoted in Eamon Duffy (ed.), *The Heart in Pilgrimage* (Bloomsbury, 2014), p. 273.

9   St Thérèse of Lisieux, *Story of a Soul* (ICS Publications, 1996), p. 189.

10   George Herbert, *The Complete English Poems* (Penguin, 2004), p. 178.

11   Simone Weil, *Waiting for God* (Harper Collins, 2009), p. 27.

12   St John of the Cross, 'Living Flame', Stanza 3, verse 28.

13   Gregory of Nazianzus, *Festal Orations*, p. 123.

14   St Thérèse of Lisieux, *Story of a Soul*, p. 189.

15   St Thérèse of Lisieux, *Story of a Soul*, p. 189.

16   St Teresa (tr. John Dalton), *The Interior Castle* (T. Jones, 1852), p. 199.

17   An episode described in *Legend of the Three Companions*, section 1,413.

18   Accessed via **catholicireland.net/saintoftheday/st-mary-magdalen-dei-pazzi-1566-1607**.

19   St Thérèse of Lisieux, 'Act of oblation to merciful love', appendix to *Story of a Soul*, p. 276.

20   Anonymous, *The Cloud of Unknowing* (Penguin, 1982), p. 61.

21   *The Cloud of Unknowing*, p. 67.

22   Duffy, *The Heart in Pilgrimage*, p. 456.

23   Isaac Watts, 'When I survey the wondrous cross' (1707).

24   *The Cloud of Unknowing*, p. 68.

25   Mother Julian of Norwich, *Revelations of Divine Love*, p. 173.

26   Alicia Ostriker (ed.), *William Blake: The complete poems* (Penguin, 1977), p. 127.

27   St Augustine of Hippo, *Confessions*, book X, chapter XXVII.
28   K. Mochulsky and M.A. Minihan, *Dostoyevsky: His life and work* (Princeton University Press, 1973), p. 152.
29   John Behr, *Asceticism and Anthropology in Irenaeus and Clement* (Oxford University Press, 2007), p. 117.
30   Quoted in Michael Harter (ed.), *Hearts on Fire* (Loyola Press, 2014), p. 8.
31   Maureen McCabe, *I Am the Way: Stages of prayer in Saint Bernard* (Cistercian Publications, 2012), p. 45.
32   St Augustine of Hippo, *Confessions*, book X, chapter XXVII.
33   Quoted in Jeanie Gushee and David Gushee, *Yours Is the Day, Yours is the Night* (Thomas Nelson, 2012), p. 210.
34   St Augustine, Homily IX in *The Nicene and Post-Nicene Fathers*, vol. VII (Eerdman, 1983), p. 518.
35   Quoted in Duffy, *The Heart in Pilgrimage*, p. 215.
36   The third letter of St Clare to St Agnes of Prague.
37   Olivier Clément, *The Roots of Christian Mysticism* (New City, 1993), p. 79.
38   A. Smith (ed.), *The Complete English Poems* (Penguin, 1996), p. 315.
39   Herbert, *The Complete English Poems*, p. 34.
40   Father Joseph P. Whelan SJ (1932–94). Talk to the Communities, Maryland Province, 1981–82. Reproduced by kind permission of the Corporation of Roman Catholic Clergymen. (Often incorrectly attributed to Father Pedro Arrupe SJ.)
41   Duffy, *The Heart in Pilgrimage*, p. 456.

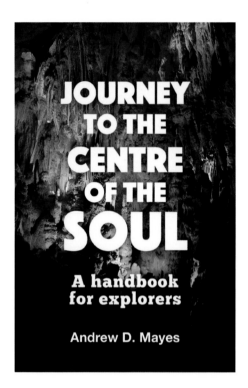

This unique and groundbreaking book is a summons to a subterranean spiritual adventure, an odyssey of the soul. If you let it, it will invigorate and inspire a search for something deeper in the spiritual life, and will link you with trusted spiritual guides to support you as you progress in a journey of discovery. *Journey to the Centre of the Soul* mines the rich seams of Christian spirituality, risks the depths, faces the darkness and make astonishing, transformative discoveries.

Journey to the Centre of the Soul
A handbook for explorers
Andrew D. Mayes
978 0 85746 582 5 £8.99

brfonline.org.uk

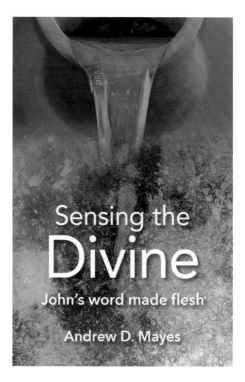

This compelling, inspiring book is an invigorating rereading of the fourth gospel. Uniquely, it approaches John's gospel by exploring how he uses the senses, both physical and spiritual, in his encounter with Jesus Christ, the Word made flesh. This refreshing appreciation of the gospel will activate and stimulate our own discoveries and spiritual quest, not only of the gospel, but also of God's world, ourselves and our mission.

Sensing the Divine
John's word made flesh
Andrew D. Mayes
978 0 85746 658 7 £10.99

brfonline.org.uk

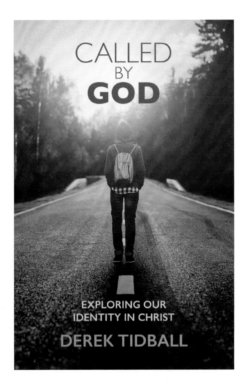

This book examines twelve key New Testament texts which speak of the Christian's calling. In days when much is spoken about vocation, this draws us back to see how the Bible speaks about the nature of Christian vocation. Each chapter ends with reflections and discussion material.

Called by God

Exploring our identity in Christ
Derek Tidball
978 0 85746 530 6 £7.99

brfonline.org.uk

Praying
the Way

with Matthew, Mark, Luke and John

Terry Hinks

Through raw and authentic prayers, based on the gospel stories, Terry Hinks leads readers into the heart of the gospels the more clearly to see the needs and joys of today's world. This highly original book helps readers to pray out of, and with, the words of Jesus and to discover the joy of prayer as a two-way conversation – listening as much as speaking to God.

Praying the Way
with Matthew, Mark, Luke and John
Terry Hinks
978 0 85746 716 4 £10.99

brfonline.org.uk

Transforming
lives and communities

Christian growth and understanding of the Bible

Resourcing individuals, groups and leaders in churches for their own spiritual journey and for their ministry

Church outreach in the local community

Offering two programmes that churches are embracing to great effect as they seek to engage with their local communities and transform lives

Teaching Christianity in primary schools

Working with children and teachers to explore Christianity creatively and confidently

Children's and family ministry

Working with churches and families to explore Christianity creatively and bring the Bible alive

parenting for **faith**

Visit **brf.org.uk** for more information on BRF's work

brf.org.uk

The Bible Reading Fellowship (BRF) is a Registered Charity (No. 233280)